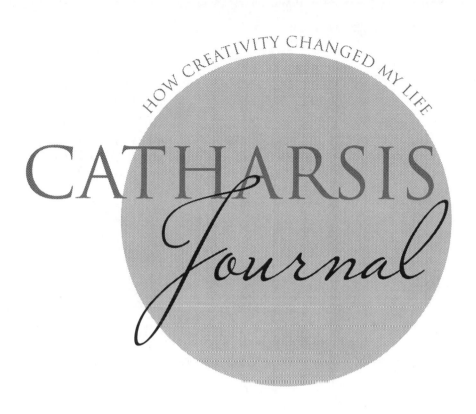

HOW CREATIVITY CHANGED MY LIFE

CATHARSIS
Journal

KRISTA BURLAE, EDITOR

BALBOA.
PRESS

A DIVISION OF HAY HOUSE

Balboa Press books may be ordered through booksellers or by contacting:

Balboa Press
A Division of Hay House
1663 Liberty Drive
Bloomington, IN 47403
www.balboapress.com
1-(877) 407-4847

Because of the dynamic nature of the Internet, any web addresses or links contained in
this book may have changed since publication and may no longer be valid. The views
expressed in this work are solely those of the author and do not necessarily reflect the
views of the publisher, and the publisher hereby disclaims any responsibility for them.

The author of this book does not dispense medical advice or prescribe the use of any
technique as a form of treatment for physical, emotional, or medical problems without the
advice of a physician, either directly or indirectly. The intent of the author is only to offer
information of a general nature to help you in your quest for emotional and spiritual well-
being. In the event you use any of the information in this book for yourself, which is your
constitutional right, the author and the publisher assume no responsibility for your actions.

Any people depicted in stock imagery provided by Thinkstock are models,
and such images are being used for illustrative purposes only.
Certain stock imagery © Thinkstock.

Printed in the United States of America.

ISBN: 978-1-4525-7994-8 (sc)
ISBN: 978-1-4525-7995-5 (e)

Balboa Press rev. date: 9/4/2013

TABLE OF CONTENTS

First Place Winner
Through the Open Door: A Bipolar Attorney talks
Mania, Recovery, And Heaven on Earth 1
Hilary M. Chaney
Arkadelphia, AR

Second Place Winner
Writing, Another Form of Music In Sonata-Allegro Form.............. 25
Lucille Joyner
Franklin Lakes, NJ

Third Place Winner
Gifts, A Story And A Memoir Of Moving On................................. 43
Jae Hodges
Huntsville, AL

Fourth Place Winner
Ahead of the HOPE... 53
Marsha Fisher
Waterloo, Iowa

Fifth Place Winner
Mourning Pages... 65
Lesley Pearl
Chicago, IL

Sixth Place Winner
The Miracles of Life, Modern Medicine, and Ancient Healing 75
Laura Brown
Parkdale, OR

Seventh Place Winner

Creativity Changed My Life 89

Annie Riess

Unity, Saskatchewan. Canada

A Tie for Eighth Place Winner

Creativity—Ticket to a Better Place 99

Julia Gregor

Concord, CA

A Tie for Eighth Place Winner

The Goddess Wakes 107

Angela La Voie

Centennial, CO

Ninth Place Winner

In Retrospect 117

Kay Learned

North Tonawanda, NY

EDITOR'S NOTE

Creativity has long been a tool of cathartic healing in a myriad of ways. A lost and undervalued attribute in today's culture, it thrives at *Catharsis Journal*. We believe in actively using creativity to nurture the experience of living with all of its ups, downs, rights and wrongs, failings and achievements and experiences that shake our foundation or glorify our existence.

The following stories are a collection of winning entries in a contest entitled, *How Creativity Changed My Life*. Each of the winning entries tells a tale of rich creative living that changed the path of the writer, healed a wound, physical or emotional, opened doors or altered a life by use of creativity. The writers are awesome to consider when you read their stories.

Within these pages are true tales of ancient healers offering modern day miracles, savage grief turned to artistic expression and disabling disorders turn to highly functioning order, all through the use of creativity. If you feel compelled to contact one of the writers, you may contact us at info@catharsisjournal.com. We will forward your request to the writer.

Congratulations to the winners of the competition!

Krista Burlae, Founder of Catharsis Writing Institute

THROUGH THE OPEN DOOR: A BIPOLAR ATTORNEY TALKS MANIA, RECOVERY, AND HEAVEN ON EARTH

HILARY M. CHANEY
ARKADELPHIA, AR

I am a Social Security Disability attorney. I just won another case for a client with Bipolar Disorder. I have a soft spot for her myriad of problems: psychotic breaks, commitment to psychiatric hospitals, hallucinations, deep depression, panic attacks . . . you name it. I felt such gratitude when I won the case. For so many clients Social Security Disability benefits just means they get health insurance and medications. For some it means they can just buy diapers for a baby. For all it means they can deal with their illness in a healthy way and get the professional treatment they need, the same type of treatment that could prevent the next tragic school shooting.

Needless to say today was a glorious day when I feel proud of my profession and lucky that I have found somewhere to do good while living with a mental illness.

Yes, living with a mental illness. I am thirty-seven and was diagnosed with Bipolar Disorder in February 2000.

I had always been a go-getter, an overachiever. In high school I was a three sport athlete and co-captain, and a straight A student. I was accepted to Princeton, Duke, and UVA. I went to Washington and Lee University in Lexington, Virginia on a full academic scholarship and

I captained the volleyball team for two years, earning all-conference honors all four years. The future could not have been brighter.

I graduated from W&L in 1998 and started working at Capital One as a project manager. I dove in to all the perks of being a grown up. Got my own apartment, bought a car, found a group of friends and had a good time with the nice salary I was drawing.

Then life started to speed up. I started to party too hard and stay up too late. I spent a bit too much money. By New Year's 1999 I had started the skid that follows a flight too close to the sun. My job started to suck. My boyfriend was not right for me, and I realized I was unhappy with most of what was going on in my life. The stress from being unhappy seemed to swallow me whole. As an aside, though I realized eventually my boyfriend was not the man for me, he performed very admirably in the very difficult months to come. I do owe him a debt.

Out at a local restaurant on Valentine's Day 2000, a Monday, I ordered my favorite Italian dish and engaged in the usual small talk, but found I had no appetite. I was not nauseous, but nervous. That night I could not sleep. I couldn't explain what was brewing in me, but something stormed all right.

The next day I went to work. I was distracted, and again I could not eat. I was tired, but energized. I felt sharp, wired, caffeinated. As I lay down to bed that night, I wondered where my mind was going. It felt unharnessed, like it had jumped its tracks. Racing thoughts . . . spinning gears . . . the documents in my brain's hard drive were shuffling and re-shuffling like a deck of cards.

I went to work on Wednesday having had no sleep since Sunday night. I kept reassuring myself that it was no big deal. People operated on little or no sleep all the time, right?

I actually felt pretty effective at work. Multi-tasking came naturally. I felt so productive that at 2:45 a.m. Thursday morning, I got in my car and drove to Capital One and worked for a good two hours at a frantic pace. That was the last I saw of Capital One for over a month.

On Thursday, which marked four days with no sleep, I begin having bizarre thoughts. I felt like I was very close to Jesus and God. In my sleep-deprived state, I wondered if perhaps I was Jesus? Surely the lack of sleep was playing tricks on me. How crazy it sounds to say you feel like

Jesus! But to be sure, I felt a huge capacity for love, and a tremendous empathy for those around me. All the while, my mind continued to race and leap and somersault in a hundred different directions.

I kept trying to eat, to no avail. I couldn't even swallow. But boy, could I talk! My speech was stream of consciousness. I felt I could not talk fast enough to keep up with the rapid firing pistons in my brain.

By Friday morning I was terrified, five days and nights without sleeping or eating.

The next forty-eight hours are blurry and the chronology is inexact for me. I know on Friday afternoon we packed up my Jeep and Sean drove me from Richmond down to my hometown of Norfolk. My parents were on vacation and not due back until Saturday, so we didn't go to my house. We thought about checking me into Norfolk General Hospital, and I tried to direct him to the hospital, but I was a babbling, dehydrated, frenzied mess so we got lost. I was still feeling overhyped and excited. Though seriously impaired, my brain seemed to be revealing things to me. Looking back, it smacked of hallucination, but to me it seemed I was getting a picture of an altered reality, or of a different dimension, or of a future time, or all three.

Sean drove me past some familiar landmarks. I was so tired that I could barely peek out from under my heavy lids, but I do remember a vision that shocked the hell out of me; it was a picture of Heaven on earth. We passed a public housing project on the right, which had always looked run down and sad. The bricks were always mildewed; the grass was more dirt than grass; the people were weary and poor. There were never any children outside.

When we drove past the projects on Friday, February 18, 2000, I saw beautifully manicured lawns, and graceful trees and bright flowerboxes, and fluttering curtains and freshly painted doors, and lots and lots of kids laughing and playing in the yards. The sun shone warmly and the sky was a pure and perfect Carolina blue. And the birds! There were brilliant songbirds of every color soaring and sailing and singing in the bright sun. And there were happy mamas and proud papas and friendly neighbors; there was lots of smiling and joking and carrying on. The kids in particular waved and beamed as we drove by, and it was as if they were saying "Come on over and join the party!" Because it looked like the happiest place I had ever seen I wanted to be with them. To this day, even when I'm not manic, I still think that was my view of the future for our world, a view of Heaven on earth.

But we had no time to join the picture perfect tableau. I was about to jump out of my skin. I was sure I was dying. For some reason, we passed up the hospital and instead checked into the downtown Marriott. I didn't flinch at the cost. We just whipped out my credit card and checked in that afternoon.

The hotel room was a dark tomb that yielded no sleep. So Sean finally took me home to my parents' house. We went up to the guest bedroom and I fell on to the bed, beyond exhausted.

I tried to sleep but I was clearly beyond sleep. I visualized myself as Jesus, having come to earth 2000 years later to love those whom love forgot, to heal those hurt by human hands. I felt just like God, like I had six billion beautifully perfect but pained children, striving to access perfect love. I felt terribly sad to think there were those out there who were lost or longing, or sick or afraid. I hurt every time anyone else hurt, like a knife to my heart. That kind of pain, a kind of super-empathy, will bring you to your knees. The greatest of loves can be outright unbearable in its power.

We would find out that religiosity, or fascination with spirituality, is a marker of Bipolar. It runs absolutely wild in me.

As sick and scared as I felt, I also felt very, very lucky. Who would not feel lucky to be the one God chose to come save the world? What got me through the darkest of hours that night was my core belief in myself. The twisted ego trip that christened me the Second Coming of Christ also gave me the faith in myself that would help me survive this night and many dark nights to come. If you think you have come to save the world, suicide becomes impossibility. At my most severely depressed, when I would playfully flick at the edge of the boning knife and wonder how long it would take for me to bleed to death, I thought, "there are too many people counting on me, and waiting for me, and starved for my message, to kill myself." The Bipolar ego is actually what saved my life on many occasions.

My parents arrived from the airport sometime late Saturday morning. Mom called a family friend who was a physician. Over the phone, he told her I needed to get to a psychiatric facility as quickly as I could.

We went to Norfolk Psychiatric Center. I was catatonic at that point. Half-dead and half-alive.

After several hours, the nurses came to take me from my parents. My mother would not leave. They told her repeatedly that family could not go to the patients' floor outside of visiting hours. The nurses said they would give me a shot of Haldol and I would fall asleep and everything would be much better in the morning. But Mom WOULD NOT LEAVE ME. She would sit by my bed that night until I fell asleep. I did not realize until later that she was so indefatigable. Mothers out there, I know you would do the same.

But back to the night before I slept; I was so very weak, I could hardly walk. I made my way up to the second floor leaning on both my mother and a nurse. They kept assuring me that "all was well, that I would soon sleep for a long time, that a room was prepared for me, and that I did not have to worry or struggle or fight any more." When you think you are about to die and they tell you "your room has been prepared for you," you get very panicky, trust me. All the language they used was meant to comfort me but instead resounded like the preamble to death, like how our religions describe the end of life.

I got to the threshold of my room and I looked at my mom. She told me it was okay, to let go. The room was dark at first. I could not see anything in it. Then the nurse turned the light on and the room was suddenly very brightly lit. My eyes were so susceptible to light at that point that I could not see anything in the room, just a bright fluorescent glow. It looked and felt exactly like everyone has described: I was crossing over death's doorstep, or "going to the light."

I stepped through the threshold and collapsed on the bed. They lifted up my hospital gown and gave me a shot of Haldol. I don't know how long I slept.

The patients at the psychiatric hospital all seemed way more whacked out than me. There were two young women who would not stop laughing deliriously. There was a large older woman whose name I can't recall, but I will never forget her because when I finally checked out of Norfolk Psychiatric, she offered me two pairs of her underwear as a parting gift. "You will need these out there," she said. It was a sweet and touching gesture. I did not keep the underwear.

At Norfolk Psychiatric there was a nurse named Mary. She took special care of me. She helped me back to my room when I wandered around with no clothes on. She tried to explain to me that they were only putting me in the room with the padded walls for my own safety. I still do not know what they were protecting me from.

I would have this recurring dream that I was in outer space, in a Star Wars world. All I could see in the absolute blackness was a ladder, stretching up above me. I could not see where the ladder led, but I certainly knew death waited below. I was clinging to the bottom two rungs with all my might, dangling dangerously over oblivion and certain to be swallowed by the nearest black hole if I fell off the ladder. I would try to climb up, and would gain traction for a minute, but then I would fall back to the bottom rung, feet swinging in panic. These dreams were both waking and sleeping dreams.

I remember tossing and turning one afternoon when I was by myself in my room. I turned toward the wall and tried to force dreamless sleep. As the same Star Wars dream overwhelmed me, I heard someone come softly padding into the room. I knew it was Jesus. He sat down next to me as I lay facing the wall. He said nothing, but he put his hand on my back and patted me, gently rubbing my back. If he had spoken, he would have said "Do not worry, it will all be okay, you are safe." I did not turn to look at him. There was so much more comfort and peace in knowing he was there without challenging God by making Jesus appear in the flesh to me. After a few comforting minutes, he got up and padded out of the room. To this day, if I am lying on my side and my husband pats my back, I feel subtle aftershocks from that moment.

I did have dreams about God and Jesus, which confounded me. I was not a churchgoer at twenty-four years old. I grew up Methodist, the most laid back of all the Christian denominations, but I was your typical liberal arts educated cynic. After college, I tried a few different churches, but still felt unfulfilled and unconvinced. It was strange thus to me that in my most trying hours, I had such a visceral bond with God and Jesus.

You might think this is just another feel-good Christian story. On the contrary, as the underlying problems that plague the modern religions revealed themselves to me over the next ten years, I knew I was not a Christian. Today I don't believe there is a monotheistic God and I do not agree with organized religion. The message that has come through in my mania is that, paradoxically, Heaven on earth will come when religion as we know it is over. And if you look closely at Scripture, this is what is predicted. It's a hazy vision that stays with me when I'm sick and well both, but when manic it becomes a Technicolor reality. It's the gorgeous Heaven the Bible predicts but it's filtered through a non-believer's lens, if that makes sense.

Within a few days, the psychiatrist called my parents in and told them to be relieved. In so many words, I had the "good" mental illness. Boy, were we far gone . . . Bipolar Disorder was considered the good diagnosis?

The hospital doctors started medicating me right away with Lithium and Risperdal and Trazodone and I began seeing a psychiatrist. I spent a total of two and a half weeks in the hospital.

I took my time recovering. Mom and Dad were gentle with me. I remember my doctors told me that some Bipolars only have one episode in their lives, and I was sure I would be the very best Bipolar I could be, so my first manic break would be my last. One therapist dubbed me "the poster child for Bipolar," because I was so disciplined about taking my medication.

One of my perpetual mistakes with my illness is that I underestimate it. I always think I've been through the worst. No, I think that I've BEATEN the worst, and that only happy days lie ahead. It took me many years to realize that my illness is as organic as my body. As I combat it and learn to contain it, it grows stronger and finds alternate ways to chip away at me. It lives, and it wants to live on.

I think of Bipolar like a video game, such as Zelda, a favorite of mine from the late 1980s. Each time you unlock a new level, after hours or days of battling the enemy, a new and more fortified enemy awaits. You must be ever vigilant and never give up, and know that with perseverance you can slay the dragon.

What I am trying to say is that in April 2000, I went right back to work and jumped back into my life full-throttle, unaware of the chronic, lifelong grip Bipolar has on its victims. I pretended nothing had happened, and I did not give my brain time to recover fully. A month later, I had another manic break during a trip to Reno. Traveling between multiple time zones is difficult for those with my insomnia issues. For those who have trouble "stopping the clock," messing with the clock can prove pretty detrimental.

In the next month I kicked Sean out of my life and watched my mom beat a path from Norfolk to Richmond every weekend. I insisted I should keep working and stay in my apartment. She wanted me home under her watch, but I felt the need for independent recovery. Looking back I know that was a mistake. In the summer of 2000, I sank into a deep depression that lasted for months. The weeks went by in a slow blur; I gained weight and slept a lot and avoided friends. I am an action-oriented girl who likes challenges and creativity and inspiration and change, so moving slowly with leaden feet through my days does not suit me. I don't imagine it suits anyone.

In the fall of 2000, I made the decision to quit my job and move home, with the intention of going to law school. My therapist in Norfolk wondered whether that would be a good idea for a Bipolar. She thought it would lead to a stressful and difficult life. She warned me about the addictions that can plague attorneys. I insisted I was stable, and as is my way, I insisted I knew what was right.

I looked back over the year 2000 and saw one major manic break and hospitalization, another scary manic break in Reno, and an ongoing bout with depression. Would you take that as a sign to jump right into law school? Never mind, it's just what I did. I entered W&L law school in the fall of 2001.

I still struggled with the dead weight of depression, but I didn't know anything different because depression comes on like a thief in the night and only after you rise from its darkness do you see how pervasive it was. When depressed, you are stuck in a cruel mental suspension; you don't think things are that bad but you also don't think they can get better. So you make no great effort to change the status quo. I just kept plodding through my life. Plodding is no way to make a mark in law school.

I got a 2.28 in my first semester at Washington and Lee. It was hard to swallow for a former A-student overachiever.

The next three years were difficult to say the least, difficult, but very, very fun. I quickly tossed aside the admonition that medication and alcohol do not mix. Those were the three most expensive years of my life, what with ballooning credit card and student loan debt. My spending was out of control, and I pay for my law school days every single month now.

I have always been absolutely dedicated to taking my medication, no matter how bad it can make me feel sometimes. I am lucky in that respect. When this all blew up in 2000, I was the first one that wanted to go to the psychiatric hospital and get medicated. I was desperate to get better and believed immediately that chemicals would fix my brain. So many of you out there don't think it can get better and skip or jettison your medication. I don't think that is the way to reach a place of health. Bipolar is a chemical imbalance . . . as one friend said, "your neurons are in backwards." Homeopathic remedies just can't manage the compromised chemical circuitry. It starts with meds.

In law school I experienced side effects from Lithium and Risperdal. I felt like I was drugged . . . in a fog. I had hand tremors and coordination problems. The simplest mechanical tasks, like threading a needle or zipping a zipper, were difficult and made me feel incompetent and clumsy. My memory and concentration were poor and I had trouble with articulation and organization when writing briefs. I was also impatient when it came to work; it was hard for me to follow through on a project or even sit through a fifty-minute class to the end. Reading law is not easy, but it was particularly tough for me, so I often skipped the reading for class and embarrassed myself when I was called on by the professors.

Law school was something of a siege on my body and mind. I constantly felt like the dumb girl and tired quickly of beating my head against a brick wall. My medications never hit the sweet spot for me. The highs and lows were exaggerated at W&L.

But there were treasures in that time too. At Washington and Lee, I met my brilliant and compassionate husband Nathan, a man who does not flinch in the face of my illness. He's loved me through the very worst times, the times when I wanted to give up on everything. EVERYTHING. He won't let me throw my life or my family away, and that makes him my very own miracle worker.

Nathan and I were Heathcliff and Cathy in law school. Or Johnny Cash and June Carter, plunging weekly into the Ring of Fire. Loving so much it hurts and then hating with black venom, spewing things we never should have said, not fighting fair. He was only twenty-one when I met him, and rightly wanted to sow his oats. I knew with electricity that only happens once in your life that I would marry him. I pushed so hard in spite of our four-year age difference, to plan our future and to dream about kids. He would get frustrated at my bossiness and my big rush to lock him down. Like June Carter Cash sang, "A little bridlin' down was what [he needed]" or so I thought, but boy he sure chafed at the bridle in those early days.

We had big fights that played out in front of our friends. But we also had sweet moments, especially when we went hiking or fishing, and a brewing deep love took root. I just think I knew we were fated before Nathan did, or before he accepted the inevitable.

My grades did gradually improve in law school and I got a good job as a law clerk at the U.S. District Court in Norfolk, thanks in part to good family connections. I improvidently blew up one time at my boss, the Chief Judge of the District Court. What a mistake that was, and how rude and impertinent I was! But the Judge was careful and compassionate with me and helped me and unknowingly, recover from that mood swing. It was a good year at the Court.

I did, however, fail the Virginia bar exam. The dulled out feeling I had from the wrong medications meant I didn't want to study and couldn't understand the law when I did study. I spent more time playing volleyball in my backyard than studying Family Law or Civil Procedure. For you guys out there preparing for the bar exam, take Nathan's advice and treat it like a full time job.

Determined to follow Nathan to Arkansas, I forced myself to overcome the Lithium stupor and studied hard for the Arkansas bar exam in February 2005, squeezing in my Barbri prep course after my full workdays at the District Court. I passed the Arkansas bar exam and moved to Arkansas to marry Nathan. We married on May 27, 2006 at Ghent United Methodist Church in Norfolk, Virginia. We had a jubilant reception at the lovely Cedar Point Country Club in Suffolk, Virginia. A bevy of tried and true Arkansas friends made the long trip to Virginia to celebrate with us, and that is still so special to me. Arkansans are some of the best people on this earth.

At the reception I danced with Dad to "Feelin' Good Again" by Robert Earl Keen. It's a touching song about when things are all going your way. When luck smiles on you and your sweet love shows up at the bar unannounced: "and when I catch your eye I saw you break into a grin, it feels so good, feelin' good again." When you think you're broke, but "look into your pocket and find three twenties and a ten, it feels so good, feelin' good again." It's a song that reminds me of coming out of depression, and a time when the sun shines again after a long darkness. It's a flash of creative lyrics that foretells a future that brims and bubbles with possibility.

It's a special song for Dad and me for another reason. He's always had a deal with me that if I ever want to kill myself, I must call him first. He has taught me to never give up; those moments of "feelin' good again" will always come back around. Always, no matter how ill you are. Dad believes Heaven is here on earth, not in some fuzzy hereafter. He thinks these Robert Earl Keen moments are Heaven breaking through the veil.

Sometimes these little moments of heavenly enlightenment require coaxing to appear, but they are always waiting in the wings. Little creative goldmines, shared from one artist to another. Our glimpses of the future, of what Heaven on earth will feel like, glimpses of absolute love of self, and of others. Glimpses of the synchronicity of our lives and of how the universe works. I tear up just thinking of my love for Dad and his own boundless love for me as I write this and as "Feelin' Good Again" plays in my mind. Well shoot, I'll just turn it on Itunes right now, Pops!

After getting married, Nathan and I settled in Fayetteville, Arkansas, where I bounced from one law job to another. I was always terrified of my bosses finding out I was Bipolar. That terror crippled me and cost me three jobs as an attorney.

There were things I really struggled with as I waded my way through the Bipolar morass. One was how I always felt people were looking at me with a clinical eye. Rosemary's Baby resonates with me, because I felt like those around me, who allegedly cared for my best interest, seemed to be always looking for Bipolar symptoms. They were the "sane" ones; I was the "crazy" one. I felt like I couldn't be a normal young woman, with normal hormonal mood swings, or bouts of bitchiness, or occasional listlessness due to not knowing what I wanted to do with my life. I felt like anytime I exhibited human emotions, and told my mom about it, she was automatically in nurse mode, trying to appraise me: Did I need more meds or a trip to the psychiatrist? I felt like I wasn't allowed to feel anything that others typically feel, or express those feelings in a thoughtful way. Any divergence from absolute pluperfect behavior would be seen as a red flag of illness. I had to act a role. I had to play a part, and hide away my trembling beating heart. I had to hide the panoply of emotions that coursed through my creative, artistic bones. I felt things deeply at times, and wonder about deep and intuitive questions, like "why are we here" and "what makes us human or divine" and "what happens after death" and "how can I be so mean to someone I love with all my heart." It's like I feel things more profoundly than others and can see their pain and joy distinctly when even they cannot. But for so long I would have to hide this higher plane of emotion, so as not to seem too "Bipolary."

I also struggle with tempering my spirit. I want happiness for others more than I can bear to say. I tremble with love for others and think I know how to make them happy; I know how to nudge them into a love-filled dominion. So I have often tried to boss people into what I think is best for them; and I come off sounding preachy and condescending. I have really had to reel that in, and it's taken years of practice. I am by no means proficient yet in letting people be themselves. If I see Heaven on earth and know how to get us all there, how can I not tell you how to do it??? So hard. I'm sort of finding a place in between: where I can ask and listen and support you, but pepper my interactions with tales of my route to happiness.

A sage rabbi friend told me this: all of the religions, all of the people, are climbing the mountain to reach the happiness at the summit where truth and peace rule. We are all taking very different paths, and no one has made it to the top yet. When someone gets to the top hopefully he can light the way for others to follow, but for now we are all just putting one foot in front of the other on our own paths. The rabbi said if someone else finds it first he would still be ecstatic and want to see what that person has found. He's not concerned with what faith gets there first, just that we get there, and how we can ALL get there. I think many Christians feel their way is the only way to the truth and are unwilling to consider another view or another path. This boxes them into an indefensible corner and alienates others who would otherwise take the time to listen to the Christian perspective.

I'm sure I am not the only one to think I am talking to you all from atop the mountain. But, hot damn, Truth seems to have unveiled her silken honey hair to me.

Nathan and I wanted to get pregnant in 2007. That's a risky proposition for a Bipolar. My psychiatrist in Fayetteville told me to come off all of my medications to get pregnant. I did.

Coming off all of my medications precipitated one more trip to Heaven on earth in present day. It was in Fayetteville in August 2007. It was just mind blowing and I wish I could take you all there. I again felt the powerful currency of love, and saw the word Love illuminated on the front of my brain. It felt like sunshine was pouring forth from all of us in golden rivulets, flowing from hands and eyes and mouths. The sun seemed to be the source but it continually regenerated all over the place, peacefully pouring over everything. It felt warm but not hot. It was vibrant but not blinding. It was sunlight in motion dancing through trees, reverberating off lips, tumbling into dark and crowded places, illuminating all that had been dark. Filling every void, in everyone.

I was not "trying" to love anymore than those around me were. It was just reflexive love, as natural as breathing. There was such empathy for one another. I felt everything that was happening to other people, all of their joy, as if it were happening to me. Everyone looked like exuberant angels.

Everything worked. Everything I did and saw fit together seamlessly. I call those times "Green Light Days," because traffic seemed to part . . . everything was on time and fluid. There were no roadblocks, no hangnails or paper cuts. When in heaven I even seemed to have a bit of foresight, in that I knew things would work, and could see the puzzle pieces fit together. This wasn't just optimism or the power of positive thinking . . . it was prescience; like I saw the answers before the questions were even asked. That's not quite right . . . it's more like I knew the questions would be answered before they were even asked, but would marvel at the answers.

You know when you go to a super nice hotel and the concierge takes care of every detail so you don't encounter a second of trouble? It was like that: we were all very well taken care of. But we weren't passive at all; we were not guests. We were active owners of Heaven, making little miracles every moment. Imagine if everyone you laid eyes on was an answer to your prayers, every single person you saw made your heart's fondest wishes come true. They knew your pleasure just by looking in your eyes. You would be ecstatic to be with people. I could not wait to see the next smiling face, the next living miracle. It made me very proud to be human. It didn't seem like some strange psychedelic trip; it felt like the most natural state I'd ever been in. Would you ever want to come back from that place? Medication is what brings you back down and it can be so hard to choose stability over Heaven. I want to be there! I want you to be there! But here, with my feet on the ground, is where I belong. For now.

The Heaven I see is close and real and attainable. I envision, as if looking down from above, a rat race maze, where humans are the rats, running around frantically. Scrambling to find a way out, banging into walls, fighting and killing for food and desperate with fear. Our heads are down, our eyes are down. Just outside the maze is heaven on earth, everything we've ever dreamed of, just waiting for us. It's contemporaneous with us. It is abundant sunlight and food and safety and peace.

Here's the shocker: there is no locked door keeping us from Heaven . . . the door is wide open for us to walk out. We just can't see it because our heads our down, and it hasn't even dawned on us to lift them. We are four inches high and the maze walls are five inches high. If we just stood on our hind legs and looked up, we would see how close Heaven is and how easy it is to walk out of the maze. We could walk right "Through the Open Door." All of us. But we are down and in the dark. We are shackled by subservience to the Monotheistic God. We are throttled by the concept of original sin and the fear of going to hell. We are bound up and tied down by religion. What I've learned from my mania, and through a winding spiritual journey where I've been as close to God as you can get and then far above and beyond his earthly realm, is this: religion has been the flashlight as we stumble in the dark, but when the light comes on, we don't need the flashlight. The Heaven I have been to is post-religion, post-God. I realize we are the Gods, which is a revolutionary proposition. The Second Coming is not me; it's not a person. It's our Becoming . . . God. "Then, face to face." 1 Corinthians 13: 12.

When I get my manic flashes of heaven, it is as if I am looking down on the rat race maze, broken-hearted that Heaven is so close but the veil is still drawn. Oh how I yearn to lift that veil!

When I am in Heaven, I see both the problem and the solution as vivid as can be. They stand out in relief as in a Magic Eye 3D picture from the 1990s. The problem is religion and has been for thousands of years. But I don't look at religion with hate. On the contrary I think of it like my soft silky security blanket from long ago, a very necessary tool. I caressed the soft corners of that blanket and held it close when the fears in my dark toddler bedroom overwhelmed me. I grew up in a religious family, and religion was a fundamental part of my path. I look back with the utmost tenderness at that time when I needed the blanket to comfort me in the dark. But now that I have walked out of that bedroom into the light and joy and independence of the wide world, I do not need the security blanket. I understand from a new perspective exactly what religion's purpose was when I was young and scared and needed faith in that security blanket.

Now I have graduated from God, or from the monotheistic concept of him. I believe we are the Gods, and we are more perfect and powerful than any God-persona could ever be. Faith has been replaced with freedom, and unbridled optimism for our future.

After I came back from heaven in August 2007, I had a very active and agitated manic episode, marked by anger at my family and stress at work and frantic writing in my manic journal. I wrote forty-three pages of what felt like a masterpiece that would save the world. It felt like God was working through me and pouring revelation into me. The words flew from my fingertips. A creative well had been dammed up inside me, and it poured forth like a tidal wave. If you saw this manifesto today you would see mania on paper, with drawings and notes scribbled in margins. It smacks of Russell Crowe's work in A Beautiful Mind.

This journal is what started my healing. I would look back over my masterpiece and find comfort, and see a connection to the true Hilary. I knew it contained the beginnings of my message for the world, and over the next six years I would refine, refine, and refine further, until it was ready for consumption by a mass audience. Blogging my story was the next step, and a book based on the manic journal will follow soon.

My time in Fayetteville was hard. I never could find the right legal job. Work was work, as it should be, and there was no place for mental weakness. There was no room for any shearing of intellect or for any departure from reality in the practice of law. Lawyers do not have disabilities. For those of you out there who are practicing law while suffering mental illness, I know the hell that is your every day. I was always terrified my bosses would find out I was Bipolar, but at the same time I was desperate to shout it from the rooftops and be done with it. I felt like I was "in the closet," hiding a deep dark secret that revealed who I was at my core. I hope for a day when we can meet mental illness where it lies, because it does not discriminate by profession.

I'd like to see a hospitable work environment for those with mental illness. Full mental health coverage on insurance plans is a start. Also allowing us to work fewer hours . . . rather than eighty hours a week, maybe we work thirty-five. Sometimes flexible schedules can head off manic breaks. It would be nice to see employers allow a couple hours a month for psychiatric treatment with no questions asked. We who suffer can be tremendously effective and creative attorneys, but we just need some accommodation and understanding. It doesn't have to be the elephant in the room.

I did get pregnant in 2007. I stayed on Risperdal but tapered off my other meds. After a rough pregnancy where I had some pretty awful thoughts, I delivered my beautiful son, River Chaney, on June 20, 2008. He turned out to be the delight of my life. I didn't figure that out until December 2009, because I suffered eighteen long months of post-partum depression. My psychiatrist put me on Abilify along with Risperdal and Trazodone after I had the baby. It never quite worked like it was supposed to.

In 2008 I tried a cutting edge psychiatric therapy called neurofeedback. It works like this (as far as this lay person can describe): You go into the psychiatrist's office for a forty-minute session. The assistant tapes electrodes that are hooked into a computer onto different parts of your brain. On the screen is a series of computer games, very simple in nature. Some look like Pacman, some like Tetris. There are no hand controls, but you can play the game just by thinking about it, actually, by not thinking about it. The goal is to relax to a point where your brain plays the game without you consciously knowing you're maneuvering it. The goal for me was to increase the sleep producing chemicals in the brain and reduce the anxious, angry or generally unquiet chemicals in the brain. The more I tried to focus on winning the game, the worse I did. The game would make me drowsy and I would almost fall asleep, but then I'd have to go back to work, and try to sleep that night. It worked on some occasions.

During one session neurofeedback caused a frightening breakdown in me. My psychiatrist tried to hook up a different part of my brain to work on some other Bipolar symptoms, and within a few minutes I was rocked by extremely emotional memories of my father when I was young. In a matter of seconds, I suddenly missed him so much I felt like my head was being crushed. The tears of love for my father poured down my face and I screamed out and told the assistant to abort the game, which she did, quickly. After that experience, I stopped going to neurofeedback. I have wondered if the treatment did any damage to my tender brain circuitry. It apparently works in lab rats . . . just not sure if it worked on me.

In the beginning of 2009, I hit the lowest low for me. I was incredibly stressed at work, and felt I could not bear the pressure of keeping my illness quiet and maintaining a normal front. I was paranoid, delusional, and terrified of losing my job. I could not sleep in spite of all my meds. I would take naps in my parked car at lunch. I got to the point one day where I hid under my desk, George Costanza style, and suffered a breathless panic attack.

I remember watching March Madness during 2009. I was in horrible shape mentally. I saw those young athletic men, so happy and determined and talented, and I hoped beyond hope that I could trade places with them, at least as long as they lasted in the tournament! I saw vigor and friendship and spirit in their smiles, and I thought I was the unluckiest person in the world to be watching that joy from the other side of a TV screen.

Yes, there were thoughts of suicide then. Driving across town to work each day, I would envision plowing my car into the oncoming traffic, and thereby saving my precious son from his tormented, sick mother. How could I ever explain my illness to this sweet baby? Would he hate me for being born to a Bipolar mother? Would one of my moods catch him by the throat, and not let go? Could he ever forgive Nathan for choosing me, for choosing so poorly in a wife? For bringing an innocent life into the realm of the mentally ill?

I remember back to that time, and know it was a scary time for my parents and for Dad especially. For a few days he thought I had broken the suicide prevention deal. I simply could not talk to anyone. I could not even phrase my torment, so I did not answer calls from my parents. Dad called me each day for three days, leaving sweet and supportive messages, but on the third day, my stalwart father sounded broken. His message, in the most delicate way, reminded me about our pact. I cried when I heard it but still couldn't pick up the phone. To give voice to my desolation would somehow confirm it.

At my worst, luck intervened and I found a marvelous therapist in Fayetteville named Marie Wood. She had all the elements necessary to make each visit relaxing and rewarding. She offered a variety of hot teas upon arrival into her cozy office, which was designed in a Zen-like Asian theme. It had a pleasing little waterfall in the corner. Marie's office offered a nice window view of her second story porch, which is where she kept the bird feed that brought all manner of curious critters to her doorstep. It was refreshing to look out on the sunny panorama and see our animal kin enjoying Marie's kindness.

Marie listened well, and asked gentle questions. She did not dismiss me when I said I thought I was the Second Coming. She allowed for that possibility, taking nothing off the table during our talks. Having someone consider that I was very special broke a dam in my ravaged body, and let the pent up emotion flow free. I told her about my feverish writing and offered her a look into my journal. I told her I would love to share my message and she said, "Why don't you write a book?" Though I loved writing creatively, I had never thought of that. She gave me the chance to turn that idea over in my mind over several sessions, and her suggestion turned into inspiration that took root in my heart then and still grows today.

Marie also used a phrase that has really rescued me. She said instead of bottling up all my feeling and pain and love and crazy visions, I should "thread it out." I needed to give voice to what bloomed in me, the good and the bad. Writing and talking and dreaming were ways to thread it out. It was no longer a scary secret thanks to Marie.

Marie helped a great deal but something had to change at work, or I feared I would vaporize. The only way out that I could envision was to tell my boss I was Bipolar, which seemed in no uncertain terms like jumping off a cliff to a figurative death, but I knew it was better than actual suicide. Without consulting Nathan, who I know would have advised against it, I told my boss, the very considerate and kind Robert Rhoads. He was surprisingly understanding (his family had faced down mental illness), and it was a great relief, but my stressful work situation did not seem to improve fast enough. I was too far underwater, too sick, too tired. I quit my job to salvage my health and we moved to Arkadelphia in June 2009 to be closer to Nathan's parents, and to give me time to regain some semblance of mental health.

Luckily for me, I had a groundswell of support in Nathan and his spectacular family. I started seeing a miracle of a psychiatrist in Little Rock. She took me off Abilify and started me on Lamictal, as well as Risperdal, Trazodone and Lorazepam. I now take six different medications a day.

Within two weeks, I felt a huge difference. The clouds parted, the sun shone, and I looked forward to each day instead of dreading waking up. I regained my mental acuity and re-engaged in social activities. Best of all, I felt a tremendous bond with my lovely son.

As the weeks went on, I continued to feel better. I also gained some insights about my illness and what treatments worked for me. The great breakthrough came when I finally bought what my wonderful therapist was selling: that repression, or attempts at extermination, of my illness were utterly futile. I was born Bipolar and would always be Bipolar. I needed to give it time and space, or it would keep blowing up in my face in manic breaks. I needed to "thread it out." I needed to talk to my therapist regularly, and write in my blog about it, and share my illness with friends, who offer such great support. What looked like lunacy in my manic journal would evolve into an avocation separate and apart from being an attorney. Blogging and speaking about Bipolar means I can help other people, and that has been a tonic. For me, it's as close to a cure as you can get.

While I have gathered my strength and health again, I've also been back to Heaven some. Not for days like before, but for flashes here and there.

When I am in heaven, every sign I see or song I hear or book I read or movie I watch speaks directly to me. It is THE epitome of how I am feeling that very second. The message, even if it's just a second long clip on the radio, is written for me, right onto my soul. The universe has chosen me above everyone else as the Golden Child in that moment, and time seems to do somersaults backwards and forwards to catch me in that moment. In Heaven, there are a myriad of dimensions tumbling over each other as if in a lava lamp. Time is circular rather than linear. I call it the transcendent dimension.

I am sure you have had brief moments where songs or movies speak to you especially. But for me, this time can last for hours. Imagine the wear and tear on the inputs of your brain when you are bombarded with messages of the purest meaning every second.

I see us all as having mental helmets on our heads. There are holes in the helmet of varying sizes and number. The helmet protects our supple and sensitive brain from outside inputs that could trigger pain, disappointment, anger, frustration, or hate. The slings and arrows of this world bounce off the helmet in a healthy way when you are stable. The holes are suited perfectly for you, so that just those inputs you can handle at any given time can pierce through the helmet. Some of us are born with football helmets that are impenetrable, which I think is not a good thing. And some of us are born with fragile porous caps that hardly protect us from anything.

My helmet normally works quite well for me, but because I am Bipolar it can change form very quickly and without much warning. All of a sudden the holes become gaping chasms and everything I hear or see touches me profoundly, and my brain begins to get hot and overwhelmed. I want to feel things on a deep level but in my manic times it becomes more than I can bear. I wobble under the weight of the emotional arrows that pierce my gray matter. The super-connectivity I have to every bit of electricity and energy in the universe vibrates like a tuning fork.

I mentioned my brain feels hot when I start to get manic. It's almost like a pressure headache, but I can feel the juices up there at the top of my brain bubbling and boiling like a pot of soup on a hot stove. "My brain feels hot" is a phrase I use with my family and therapist, and when they hear that they know I need an adjustment in medication. The meds can turn down the heat on the stove. Richard Dreyfuss, a fellow Bipolar, painted a clear picture when he said there is a faucet in his brain that is either flowing too fast or too slow, and his medication moderates the chemical flow.

Giving space and voice to Bipolar and painting creative pictures of my illness is the right thing for me. How do I know this? Because my life is no longer broken. I am a Social Security Disability attorney at the Chaney family law firm, working a flexible schedule but managing a full caseload of disability clients. I do have some sleepless nights sometimes and I get stressed and sometimes paranoid, but if I can remind myself that my family supports and understands me, I feel better. When I have a few sleepless nights in a row I take an extra Lorazepam either during the day or at night. It's a PRN prescription and my psychiatrist trusts me to take it as needed based on my symptoms. She knows I will not overdo it and that I will call her if I need more help. Her office has a twenty-four-hour line by which you can reach a doctor at any time. This is such a wonderful policy for psychiatrists, and she and her colleagues are so progressive and generous in giving their time to patients.

Speaking of psychiatrists, I want all of you to know that it can take a while to find the right doctor for you. That goes for therapists too. It is like dating; you both have to like what the other is saying and how they make you feel. Goodness knows, I have had to "break up" with at least ten psychiatrists or therapists in thirteen years, and sometimes they do not take it so kindly! That in itself can be stressful and complicate your illness. But each doctor is a step in the right direction, a step toward figuring out your illness and better predicting your episodes.

I am lucky to be supremely in tune with my body and mind in regards to Bipolar, and I am the first to know when I need help. It took several years to feel comfortable asking for help, and WANTING to ask for help. And TRUSTING in the help given. Of course there is an instinct to keep the sometimes beautiful nature of mania to yourself, because you don't want anyone to steal it or dull it. They can never steal your heart. They can never steal your creative gifts. They will always reside in you and the proper medication will help you channel them into something productive. I imagine Kurt Cobain, another Bipolar, and a genius, felt that medication would still the winds of creation in his brain. He likely could not find the balance that would let him create in a healthy and glorious way. Because when you get the right recipe of medication you can paint your genius on the world canvas in the biggest way. You can become even more that you dreamed of in your manic delusions.

It took twelve long years to get the right recipe of medications. You must be vigilant and never give up trying to find the healthiest you. And you must never feel like you are alone. I am here, we are all here; a call for help is the most important first step. It all gets easier from there. But I caution you; it does not get easier overnight. There is not one magic pill that will solve all your problems instantly. Remember it took me a dozen years.

There is stress associated with my job, and pressure. I want to win for my clients. I recently argued a Social Security case in front of the 8th Circuit Court of Appeals in Kansas City, which is the Big Time. It's the highest court you can go to for these cases. Instead of being trapped by fear, or strangled by stress, I looked forward to the challenge and worked my butt off to get prepared. I can no longer wait until the last minute to do things; I have to prepare in advance and work during my sons' nap times and daycare.

I enjoy to the fullest being mother to River and Carter, and they are flourishing in many ways. I help Nathan behind the scenes in his various lines of business. I volunteer for Arkansas Judges and Lawyers Assistance Program. I teach Continuing Legal Education about my Bipolar journey. I play golf and tennis and softball. I love to cook and entertain and I thrive in the community of good people in Arkadelphia. My illness is now the backstory, not the boss.

I still see flashes of Heaven on earth, which are a sweet and ironic reminder that I am Bipolar but it can be beautiful. I know with everything I am, that we'll all get to walk in Heaven on earth soon and would be lying if I did not say I want to be the one to lead us there. As you know, that is the touchstone of mania, feeling that you are a savior. I'll never escape that mantle, and I wouldn't trade that inspiring feeling for the world. I can finally offer my message from a place of balance and peace. The creative firestorm that was the manic journal started it all, and I will publish the book soon enough.

This piece is part of a book of the same title that will be published in 2013.

WRITING, ANOTHER FORM OF MUSIC IN SONATA-ALLEGRO FORM

LUCILLE JOYNER
FRANKLIN LAKES, NJ

INTRODUCTION

My earliest exposure to writing was seeing my mother at the kitchen table copying word after word from a huge unabridged dictionary in her fierce determination to learn to read and write. I was the youngest of nine children, so my poor tired mom would often fall asleep at the aluminum kitchen table with her head on the dictionary and the old ink-filled pen still in her hand. I did not realize that this memory would be preserved somewhere in my creative reservoir and one day emerge as a writing career.

There were three main things available to me as a child: a typewriter, a piano, and my mother's sense of humor. Because women had little value beyond childbearing and keeping house, no money was wasted on girl children, so whatever I wanted to learn, I had to learn on my own.

Typing was a cinch. I followed the book and learned the right way. I also gravitated to the piano, the old monstrous Autopiano Upright that sat silently under the old stained glass window since child number two, several generations before I was born. My endless practicing made up for the years it sat there silently and, in fact, became so excessive that my mother had the piano moved upstairs so the remaining members of the family still at home could have a life.

Music took over my every waking moment. Even away from the piano, I was enveloped in a kaleidoscope of sounds. It wasn't enough to just hear all the sounds in the universe; I had to analyze every one of them. I learned to identify cars by their horns and wondered why the Volkswagen Bug and panel trucks had a single tone, and compact cars were a major or minor 3rd. I could never understand why very expensive cars had such out-of-tune triads. The dentist's drill sent out the whole overtone series spiraling from the basic perfect fifth. If you listen carefully, you can hear it in florescent lighting, also. The whole world was a glorious symphony of sounds and I wanted to hear them all.

EXPOSITION

First Theme

After years of playing the piano, I wanted to learn to read music. I lived in a city that had one of the finest music schools in the world, so one day I impulsively called there and said, "I would like to take piano lessons." The secretary asked, "Which professor?" Since I didn't know any of them, I answered, "You pick one."

I will never forget the interview with the professor. My 5'2" ninety-nine pound form stood at his solid second floor studio door knocking timidly. The door swung open and I found myself staring up at a huge big-as-life Hummel figure, with his plaid jacket and rosy cheeks, someone you might see a caricature of in The New Yorker under Famous People. He waved me in, pointed toward his Steinway B Grand Piano and bellowed, "Play!"

At this point, I had a repertoire of eight hours of classical pieces that I had learned note-for-note from records. The first piece I played for him was Chopin's Fantasie Impromptu in C-sharp minor. He told me my phrasing was excellent. I thanked him, but didn't have a clue what he was talking about. Then he asked how long I'd studied. I was too embarrassed to say never, so I answered "Two years," thinking it was a long period of time to study piano. It wasn't. It was pitifully short, but I didn't know any better.

He wanted to hear more, so I played Beethoven's Sonata Pathetique, some Debussy, and a Schumann piece. Then he said something I did not expect to hear. He said, "Why don't you register for the school?" I was taken aback and answered softly, "What do I have to do?" He said, "You have to audition, of course. You can play what you played for me, but it is required that you play a Bach Prelude and Fugue."

I had never heard of Bach. The Professor wrote down the edition he wanted me to buy, the Kalmus Edition. This marked the first time I had ever bought written music, but in keeping with my standard practice, I bought the records. I listened to them, found the Prelude and Fugue that I liked, and learned them. I still feel guilty that I let this fine gentleman believe that he taught me the Bach Prelude and Fugue in the three lessons I took from him.

Incredibly enough, neither he nor any one of the brilliant professors that made up the audition panel ever suspected that I couldn't read music. The loophole in their system was that they always tell you in advance what piece you are going to study next, so you never need to sight-read anything. There was always time to get the record.

Second Theme

While at music school, a local musician invited me to a jam session in town, so I heard Jazz for the first time. It was the complete opposite of Classical. In Classical, you play what someone else wrote. In Jazz, everything you play is your own, the arrangements, the chord changes, the improvisations, everything. YOU are the composer. Many Jazz greats did not know how to read music. Maybe that's why I identified so deeply with it. Jazz depended completely on the level of your ability to "hear" and analyze and this was where I excelled.

These jam sessions were truly a melting pot. Despite the terrible racial prejudice at the time, anyone interested in Jazz that could play an instrument was welcome in this well-known club in the black section of town. It was an opportunity for Jazz hopefuls to get the necessary experience to play professionally. It was also a way for the club owner to bring in business.

One of the Jazz hopefuls was a trumpet player named Anatole. He thought he was the Russian Miles Davis. He'd get up there on the bandstand and immediately get into the Miles stance, with his body straight, head down, and horn parallel to the floor. Actually, we were always surprised when he showed up at all as it meant that no irate husband had caught up with him yet. And there was Poco Valdez—or was it Paco?—from Mexico on guitar. That wasn't his real name, but he had things he was running from. Johnny Esposito, "the kid from Italy," practiced trumpet eight hours a day and developed a beautiful tone. He really mastered the instrument. He could even hit a clean high C. Unfortunately, he could not count to four, so quite often there would be one beat short in the measure, and this threw the rest of the band off. The tune would continue, but with everyone in a different place. Musicians were not eager to share the bandstand with him, so when they saw him coming, they'd scatter. I often wondered what field he ultimately ended up in, certainly not music.

One of the real professionals was pianist Vernon Biddle who was from the Deep South. He had traveled with some top Jazz players, like The Charlie Mingus Band, and other top names. He and other great musicians would show up from time to time to keep the sessions going.

Third Theme

Each language has its own rhythms and inflections and musicians carried it over into their improvisations. In time, I could hear a solo over the radio and know exactly what language was spoken in the home. The Jazz musician of today is not like the old naturals whose tortured soul passed through their instrument. They are schooled musicians who play a more intellectual Jazz. But then Jazz is not very much in demand today anyway, so it really doesn't matter what they do. We still have the old Greats.

After a few months of listening and analyzing Jazz, I was gigging weekends with a duo or trio in the small clubs around the center of town. There was a PhD student who used to show up at my gigs. I had no time to date and the only reason I even spent any time with him at all was that he was intelligent, talented, and he had a great sense of humor, with an emphasis on the latter. He had artistic talent and drew caricatures of politicians and stuffy upper class figures—some of them sketched on my homework assignments.

If you have a trio, as I did, you soon become aware that to a drummer, the whole word is a giant drum set, and he is known to paradiddle all over the place, even in restaurants with his knife and fork. By the same token, when you spent time with an artist, as I did with the PhD student, the whole world becomes a giant easel, and his caricatures end up everywhere, even on walls.

Codetta with New Themes Added

When PhD left town, I thought that was it. We had a lot of laughs, but we had to get on with our lives. Then he started writing me. Our letters brought with it a whole new relationship. In person, we could look at each other's facial expression and burst out laughing, but on paper it was different. You can't see expressions, so you had to spell everything out. You get to know a whole different side of a person.

One day, I received a very surprising letter from him that said, "Luce, You are the best writer I know. Get started on your autobiography." I remember thinking, "What is he talking about? I'm a musician, not a writer. And besides, what does a caricaturist know about writing, anyway?" I reasoned that it was a very nice gesture from a very nice friend and thought no more of it. Of course, I was taken aback a few years later when I saw a book written by him on the best-seller list that later became a movie. It gave me pause. He never told me that he was a writer. The subject never came up. Is it possible that he really saw something in my writing? Was I a writer? But I soon dismissed it again with, "Nah, he was just being nice."

Another Theme

While still gigging around town, a club owner hired a New York singer without letting me know. She handed me her music and when I told her that I don't read music, she panicked. I calmed her down and said, "Look, just sing the melody then go down the chord. She did this with her tunes, and we went out there and performed flawlessly. Afterwards, she said, "Do you know that there are New York musicians who cannot do what you did tonight?" She gave me her telephone number and told me that if I'm ever in New York, to look her up.

DEVELOPMENT

First Theme

By the time I was ready to move on in life, I had acquired an acoustic bass as collateral on a delinquent loan. I didn't want to take anyone's instrument, especially one that was bigger than I, but he insisted. He had four basses and said he didn't need this one. The bass and I showed up on the singer's doorstep in New York City. She had sung with the Benny Goodman band, so knew them all. One day she told me that they had just gotten in from a tour and she introduced me to one of the musicians. He was tired of the road and was quitting the band. In eight months we were married.

Theme and Variation

It was during the first year of married life that I finally took the cover off the bass to see how hard it was to play. As a pianist, I could never find a good bassist and I wondered why. Was bass that hard to play? I found it so incredibly easy that after exploring the instrument for about a month, I was hired to play bass in an all girl group called The Satin Dolls. There seemed to be more of a need for bass players than piano players at the time.

In this group, I never learned the names of the beautiful standards that we played. They were never called out. All the vibes-playing leader did was to hold up fingers to tell us what key it was in, and after that, we were on our own.

Second Theme

Also, during this first year of married life, I received a letter with a censorship stamp on it from a low-security prison. It's where men were sent for possession of marijuana so, this man wasn't a dangerous criminal or anything, he was simply a musician.

Being so allergic, I was the only musician at the jam sessions back home who did not smoke marijuana, and since I was the only woman at these sessions, I had to find ways to avoid all the musicians' raging libidos. I quietly allowed many misapprehensions about me to stand uncorrected. They gave me a cover.

There was terrible racial prejudice at the time. Although all races were free to go to the sessions, there was this underlying belief that it was OK for the guys to be friendly with the black musicians, but not a girl. When I was friendly, rumor had it that I was going with a black musician. I let it stand. It made the white guys back away and I could just enjoy the music. I invited a female sax player to the sessions, and the new rumor was that I was a Lesbian. Now everyone backed away and life was even better for me at the jam sessions.

Prejudice worked both ways. The club owner once apologized to me because the chef would not make a hamburger for me. I never knew if it was because I was white, or because he thought I was a Lesbian. Generally, the owner was not that happy to see me there, either, since I didn't drink and would nurse a soft drink for four hours. Everyone finally understood that I was there for the music and learned to just tolerate me.

The prisoner heard about me from a bass player who knew me from the jam sessions. In fact, he tried to steal my bass once. Nonetheless he had a high regard for me as a musician. There's nothing like being held in high esteem by your burglar. The letter writer was languishing in prison without a musical instrument and wanted someone on the outside who understood his situation to try to find a sax or a clarinet for him. I went to every charitable organization I could find, to no avail, but the prisoner and I continued to correspond anyway.

Theme and Variation

My letters to him were my second extended letter writing experience. The first was the PhD student after he left town, and the prisoner, my second. Writing was easy for me, and being in a band and playing in the different clubs plus private parties, there was a lot to write about, so I poured it all out in letters. I remember writing him about a private party that I'll never forget.

It was at the home of a New York East Side heiress who threw a party for her friends at The New Yorker. They were a very funny lot. One cartoonist earnestly insisted that his cat had a vocabulary of fifty-four words. He also talked about his discovery of keeping your hands warm in the winter by slipping them in your armpits. Another cartoonist was Charles Addams, creator of The Addams Family cartoons and movie. He looked just like one of his characters in his long black coat and gaunt look. He didn't speak very much, just hung around, like a dark shadow, listening to what everyone else was saying. So did I, actually.

I wondered where the hostess's husband was, but he was not around. I later learned that she was in the process of divorcing him, and while he still lived there, he was not invited to the party. She openly informed everyone that she was divorcing him because he refused to stop his bedtime flatulence. What's more, he would pull the covers over her head when he did this. I got the distinct impression that he didn't like her very much. I could hardly keep a straight face throughout her candid soliloquy, but her artistic friends simply listened and saw it as justifiable grounds.

When the husband came home and saw that a party was going on, he stepped in, gave us all a dirty look, and retreated to his own room. The music was too loud for us to hear whether he spitefully crepitated at us as he passed.

Theme and Variation

The interesting thing that happened during this year of letter writing was that George, the prisoner's censor whose job it was to check incoming and outgoing letters for illegal stuff, became obsessed with my letters. Whenever he returned to work from vacations or sick days, he would ask to read any of my letters that he missed, even though his sub had already checked them. He never asked to read anyone else's. George apparently saw something in my letters, so now I had an audience of two and I thoroughly enjoyed it. I didn't realize it at the time that events like this served to prepare the groundwork for a new discipline that would one day open up for me.

When this musician was paroled, it marked the end of an era for me. I had grown so dependent on this captive audience that it was a loss when it was over. Fortunately, he had saved all of my letters and was kind enough to return them all to me. I plan to read them one day. I'm sure there's a book in there somewhere.

Retransition

When I married, I had been so wrapped up in music, I had virtually no dating experience, and so my judgment was flawed. I assumed that because my husband was a successful musician, he must love music the way I did. I was way off. Our talents were totally opposite.

He mastered the horn and could read anything, so he was in demand for all the high paying jobs in the music industry. He could sub in a Broadway Show cold and cut the show perfectly. I still hear good reports about him though he's long since been dead. He ultimately took a coveted staff job at CBS where he worked one full day a week and earned what it took the average person a full year to earn at a nine-to-five job. What's more, if he worked more than six hours on that one day, he got overtime. It gave him a lot of money and a lot of free time. He was free to do commercials, beauty contests, or whatever turned up. But I noticed that to him, music was a job that he did successfully, but I never got the impression that he loved music. If he had a few days off, it was spent watching TV Westerns while the horn stayed in the closet. I never said anything, but I really couldn't understand it.

On the other hand, I could not live without my music. Because a piano would not fit in our two-room New York apartment, I continued my music on bass. It was the music that I loved, not the instrument. I often felt that if my husband and I were ever stranded on a desert island, he would just sit there and wait for death, whereas I would find a way to make music, whether it was with seashells or a hollowed out tree trunk. I'd find a way.

We played one dance gig together and it was so embarrassing, we never mentioned it again. He simply could not play without music, not even an old standard melody, and the humiliation was too much for him. He was so used to success and adulation he could not accept being upstaged by someone who couldn't even read music.

Little by little, my keen musical ear began to annoy him. If we were driving along and a tune came on the radio, by the time we got home, I had it memorized and could play it. My brain was so attuned to music, that there was nothing I could not hear and reproduce. Once, I even learned a song in my sleep. The TV was on and I heard a beautiful tune. I awoke without opening my eyes and just lay there listening and analyzing. The tune bombarded my mind the whole day and I had no peace until I sat at the piano and played it. It took six months or so before I could find the name of the movie that it was in. The tune was, "I Hadn't Anyone Till You," and the movie was, "In A Lonely Place" with Humphrey Bogart. When it was on TV again, I was amazed to find that I had learned it in the same key that the sultry singer sang it in.

My husband's resentment began eating away at the marriage. If I sat at the piano and started playing, he'd automatically turn the radio on so that I couldn't hear myself and had to stop. Despite how it looked, I don't think he did it deliberately. It was subconscious. He simply couldn't handle it. And since he was home a lot, I had very little opportunity to play piano. In effect, the marriage marked the end of my music. It was disheartening to see that this marriage did not become the two-part harmony that I expected. I turned to my typewriter and expressed myself in letters to my very close friend who was also married to a musician. I wrote her every funny thing that happened, every tragic thing that happened, everything. I made copies and saved them all as a form of diary. It never occurred to me at the time that these letters would one day prove to be valuable to my writing.

Closing Section

In our twelfth year of marriage, when my son was ten and my daughter was five, the marriage was over. My husband dropped out of sight in another state, and I found myself with total support of a household. In my split-level, I separated the rec room from the rest of the house with double doors, made two entries through the garage and rented it out. That covered the mortgage and taxes. Since I had always tuned my own piano, I went into piano tuning. With my own business, I was able to arrange my schedule around my children's schedule without the expense of sitters.

Final Theme

It was a very busy time of my life, juggling lives and finances and working as much as I could. While I yearned for my music, I didn't have the energy to practice after such full days. Also, with tenants downstairs and children sleeping, I didn't want to disturb anyone. The only thing I could do quietly and effortlessly was to sit at my kitchen table and write letters. Perhaps, I was destined to sit at the kitchen table like my mother and learn to write.

RECAPITULATION

First Theme

One day, I was incensed over a parking regulation that seemed to favor some people over others. It was an inconvenience and expense to my family and I needed to know who was responsible for such an Ordinance. For the first time in my life, I wrote a letter to the editor. To my surprise, my letter got the attention of the Mayor—our first female Mayor. She had nothing to do with the injustice, but actually ran for office to correct injustices. She straightened out the matter and I ended up being her ghostwriter. I wrote her letters, campaign literature, and speeches. It was a strange new experience to hear my words coming out of someone else's mouth. It was even stranger to watch people congratulate her after giving a speech that I had written and then say, "I can see why you were elected mayor."

To better understand the mayor's challenges and help her more, I attended council meetings. That was a big concession for me, a person who can't stand meetings. And what made them so excruciating was not only the endless quibbling over minutiae, but the behavior of a chauvinistic councilman who could not accept a lady mayor. He particularly hated this one because she refused to do underhanded things that would benefit him, and he did everything he could to debase her publicly at every meeting. He single-handedly caused the council meetings to last five hours because of his time-consuming sarcasm and lunatic ravings against the Mayor. This man was beyond offensive. He needed to be committed.

Finally, at one meeting, the councilman pushed it a little too far. The Mayor said, "We will now have a moment of silent prayer" instead of "We will now have a moment of silence." That councilman pounced on this like a lion bagging a deer and he would not let it go. He carried on in a childish rampage of insults and accusations to make it look like she deliberately intended to defy the law by using the word prayer. It resulted in another five-hour meeting.

I was so disgusted with this man, I wrote a letter to the editor, saying, "At last night's council meeting, the mayor inadvertently said, 'We will now have a moment of silent prayer' instead of just 'a moment of silence.' The only one who objected to it, and made an issue of it, was Councilman So-and-so. Let's hope that when he is up for re-election next week that he doesn't have a prayer." This was a small town with many churches. The councilman lost the election.

First Variation on a Theme

After I started writing for the mayor, the editor of a local paper called and asked me to do a column. Having no experience, I followed my natural bent toward humor and my column turned into humorous depictions of all sorts of local situations, especially councilmen, whom I facetiously referred to as "clowncilmen."

One of my stories was a fictional account of an actual event. Because of the chauvinistic resistance by the male department heads, no one would cooperate with the mayor. She couldn't get anyone to scoop up a dead raccoon near the municipal building because they all responded testily with, "It's not my job!" She finally just got a shovel and a plastic bag and cleaned it up herself. Then they all ganged up on her, looking for any reason to bring her up on charges, but they had no basis for it. She did everything absolutely legally correct in the disposal of a carcass, so there was nothing they could do.

This whole situation was so ridiculous, I wrote a story paralleling it called, "The Council Meeting." It was about a dead bird on the border of two towns and it was attracting a crowd from both towns, each of which did not know whose responsibility it was to dispose of the bird. In the story, the dead bird problem is brought before our Mayor and Council for resolution, and I accurately applied each councilman's personality and bizarre responses to the problem in their clumsy search for a solution.

Town reaction to this story was phenomenal. Though I never mentioned any names, the whole town figured out the identity of each councilman. We all knew exactly how each one would react to such a situation. One woman wrote that she and her husband were laughing so hard they could hardly get through it.

After a year, the paper folded. Someone who was connected with the newspaper absconded with the funds, and after that, the editor died, and that great experience was over.

Second Variation on a Theme

One day I happened to come across a discounted anthology of American Humor by Russell Baker. It must have been in a supermarket, because I had no time to browse around bookstores. His picture was on the back cover and he looked familiar, plus I wanted to see what the different authors considered humor. Part of my interest was that as

I thumbed through the pages, I came across a bit of humor by my PhD friend from the past, the first person to tell me I was a writer.

I was so happy to find a book on humor that I wrote the author a note expressing my gratitude for his book. I didn't know how to contact the author, so I addressed it to his publisher and hoped it would reach him. Just before I sealed the letter, I impulsively inserted a copy of my story, "The Council Meeting." After I mailed it, I did not give it another thought. I wasn't expecting anything. My mind and body were too exhausted to think past the duties and pressures of each day.

Around a month later, to my surprise, I received a letter from him. One sentence is indelibly etched on my soul. He said, "You have talent for satire." It reminded me of when that music school professor said that my phrasing was excellent and I thanked him but didn't have a clue as to what it really meant. Here, I understood "talent" but didn't have a clue what satire was.

I tended to put things in two categories: Humorous or Serious. I did not know the finer shades of Humor, one of which is Satire. I had to look it up. It meant that my story was not just humor in which a comic figure falls down the stairs and makes people laugh. It meant that my story was in the category of "A literary work that uses wit, irony, or sarcasm to expose and discredit vice or folly." I was ecstatic.

I also looked up his biography, then thought, Imagine! A two-time Pulitzer Prize winner says I have talent for satire. Maybe my writing does have Merit. Maybe I should have taken that PhD friend seriously in the first place.

Third Variation on a Theme

My piano tuning business was growing and I was in and out of three to four homes a day. Humorous stories were all around me and I wrote down as many as I had time for. In fact, there was humor before I even got into the business. The very first call on my Ad was from a woman in the next town who was giving me directions to her dance studio. She said, "You get on Mountain Ave, go left at Central, turn left at the first traffic light, go to the third house on the left, the one with the wrap-around porch. Go up the stairs and climb in the window to the left of the doorway. I'll leave the window unlocked for you." That's all I needed was to be caught climbing in a window carrying a black bag.

Once the children were in bed, I wrote up many of these humorous experiences. One story was about the late Roger Baldwin, founder of the ACLU. My earlier job ran late, so I didn't have time for lunch. Mr. Baldwin asked, "Would you care for some cheese and crackers?" I said I would, but then he disappeared. In time, my hypoglycemia was kicking in, so I decided to go look for him. I wanted to do a great job on his old Knabe Upright, but I couldn't if I my energy was so low.

I found him at a meeting in his living room with some very well dressed, important-looking people. All heads turned to look at me when I entered the room. They were expecting a message that had to be vital enough, like a phone call from the president, to merit disturbing this extremely important meeting. Instead, they hear, "Mr. Baldwin, where is my cheese and crackers?" The expressions on their faces were priceless. All heads turned toward Mr. Baldwin in anticipation of annoyance, but instead, he said, "Oh, yes. I'm sorry," and he jumped up and ran to the kitchen and got me my cheese and crackers.

Guitarist Les Paul was another funny tuning job. When he called me, he used his real name, so I didn't know who he was. I was trying to tune his piano and he wouldn't stop talking about all the famous people he knew. I figured he was a delusional old millionaire who watched too many black-and-white movie classics. I was on a schedule, so had no time to talk. By the time he got to Claudette Colbert, I put down my tuning hammer and said, "This is very interesting, Mr. Polsfuss, but would you please go in the other room so that I can finish this piano?" He stared at me for a moment, then turned on his heels and left. On the way home, I suddenly realized who he was. He was that music legend who invented the multi-track recording and the solid body electric guitar. This man single-handedly launched the rock movement. I figured he would never call me again after kicking him out of his own studio, but I was wrong. He did, in fact, call, and I tuned his piano for at least twenty years or more after that, right up to his death.

Fourth Variation on a Theme

One of the stories that led to another turning point in my writing was "The Piano Sale." A man wanted to surprise his bride-to-be with a piano. It was a Friday night and the piano had to be delivered and tuned that very night if it was to be there by the wedding. The details of this sale and the delivery across a lake in pitch black darkness on a pontoon with two Hungarians were so hilarious that I brought a copy of it to edit while my car was being serviced. I was laughing so hard, that the woman who ran this family business came over to me and, with a smile on her face, asked me what I was laughing at. Rather than explain it to her, I handed her the manuscript and she read it for herself.

Ten months later, she called me up and said, "We have decided to put out a newsletter for the business. Would you mind giving me a copy of that story you wrote about that piano? I'd like to run it in the newsletter." I remember my saying, "What has a piano got to do with cars? She said, "Don't worry about it. I just want some humor in the newsletter."

I thought it was a onetime thing, but she called the following month for another story and the following month after that. Pretty soon, she wasn't asking, she was expecting. I ended up giving her a story a month for three years, until her newsletter venture was over. It was a great experience and I loved every moment of it, especially the feedback from her and her clients.

Second Development

Music was my first love and while it was so rudely snatched from my life, I thought it was gone forever. But it wasn't. That gene had passed into my daughter, whom I knew was a musician even before she was born. I would play a bass note against my bulbous abdomen, and she'd respond with a kick. Then when she was six weeks, three days old, she was able to match a tone sung or played to her, which shocked everybody to no end. Babies normally do not have the vocal control to do this. Then when she was older, she crawled over to the piano, pulled herself up on the piano leg, made her way to the center of the piano, and while hanging on with the left hand, she played "Mary Had A Little Lamb" over her head with her right hand. Then in school, her kindergarten teacher took me aside once and said, "My husband didn't believe that I had a child in my class who could play piano, so I recorded her. Now he believes it." My daughter confirmed the transfer of this gene to her soul when she said, "If I couldn't ever have my music, I wouldn't want to live."

Once, when I told my daughter that when I think of my mother, I see her at the kitchen table fast asleep with her head on the dictionary and the pen still in her hand, she answered, "That's strange, Mom. When I think of you, I think of you fast asleep on the couch with an open dictionary on your chest."

CODA

There are still times when I grieve my lost music, like a mother who grieves for the beautiful baby lost in childbirth. But that doesn't mean that there isn't enough love left for the next child.

Little by little, I came to see writing as another form of music. The creative process is much the same. You're still painting a picture, except that instead of using tones, you're using words, words that are in themselves small units of music with their own sounds and rhythms.

In the past, I saw music everywhere. Today, I see stories.

GIFTS, A STORY AND A MEMOIR OF MOVING ON

JAE HODGES
HUNTSVILLE, AL

I stand here, day after day, in this kitchen with its bare white walls; at this sink empty of any signs of living; just below this window, that looks out over a somber yard. There are rigid curtains, colorless, not even a flutter in the dead air. I am so accustomed to seeing emptiness around me that I am untouched by the totality of utter blankness outside. What should have been spring has melted into one long season called Solitude. I stand here washing dishes. Dishes for two, used one at a time: a plate here on the counter, later a bowl in the sink, finally a half empty wine glass. All these months . . . it's always the same, day after day after day.

Soap bubbles hide my red and chapped hands, and the simple tarnished wedding band. My mind replays our conversation this morning, every morning, a ritual that now haunts me, day after day.

"You will do something today." He holds his hat with both hands, close to his body, another barrier between us. Not a twitch, not a wink, not a black hair out of place. Over the years he's become a statue when he talks to me; talks at me. And I have allowed him to do it. But this time is different; I am different. I'm resolved not to answer, not to give him what he wants, this time. Today, I break the cycle. For once, the silence pounds away his voice from my ears.

Then he walks away. Just walks away.

So, here I find myself standing at the kitchen sink, staring out the window, a day like every other day . . . every other day . . . almost.

I no more notice that snow is now falling . . . falling hard . . . than I noticed the flowers blooming just minutes ago, or maybe it was hours, or days. The swing set I'd had built is completely blanketed by the thick coverlet of snow. Somewhere out there, buried deep beneath all that empty whiteness is a young woman, gently swinging back and forth, a new baby in her arms, a content smile at her lips. I wash, and rewash, each dish and utensil only to prolong the task. This is what I have to do today.

A distant chime breaks the spell, and I drop the crystal glass I've been soaking, scrubbing, rinsing, drying . . . over and over again. It falls, in slow motion, to the floor and I watch, mesmerized, as the leaded glass shatters in silence and bits of it spray in all directions. And still I watch, as the floor around my bare feet becomes a pool of colors careening in the morning sunlight.

The mailman, of course; who else would be coming to my door in the morning, during the week, when everyone has something to do? He has a kind face and he tips his hat everyday, without fail, a small dose of comfort.

I'm in no particular hurry. I push down on the faucet, and interrupt the steady flow of water, then pull the pink towel from my shoulder to dry my hands while I turn toward the front of the house. I trudge across the shards; I've already forgotten about the broken glass. The larger pieces, closer to the crash site, gouge at the bottoms of my feet. Further out, miniscule slivers find their way into the open wounds. I leave a trail of red footprints, like breadcrumbs to help me find my way back.

I throw open the door—no fear—only to find left behind, at the top of the porch steps, a lone box. I step out to the edge of the porch, then down the four narrow steps. The frost bites at my open wounds as I make the first impressions in the virgin snow, cherry snow cones melting under a summer sun. The street is empty as far as I can see in all directions.

The box is big enough that I need both hands to pick it up, but light enough that I could toss it all the way to the curb and be done without another thought. It's wrapped in plain brown paper with the usual express mail stickers. The cancellation is typically hurried and half smudged; no name and a simple post office box in a large city where I can think of no one that I know.

Back in the kitchen, I feel the warmth of the room around me. I stand defiant, my back to the window that frames the world of endless white, and put the package on the table. I don't reach for knives anymore. Instead, I work a single finger into the layers of paper, easily ripping the paper open and then off the package; discarded to the floor.

The box inside is unmarked, and the cardboard is heavy; it doesn't give at all under pressure from my fingers. Drawn to the slit in the top of the box, held together with a single piece of packing tape, I remember a time when my childish and vulnerable hands had fallen under the spell of an old Ouija board. Excitement ignites within them now just as it had then, and it occurs to me that the only reason that anyone would possibly have for sending me a gift is gone. Who'd I neglected to tell? Who had missed the news that my daughter had died so shortly after she'd opened her perfect eyes to a less than perfect world?

I can't open this; I can't torture myself. I won't give in. Maybe he's right; maybe I need to put this behind me and move on. Maybe this package belongs in the trash as a pledge to myself to do just that. Just steps to the trashcan. Lift the lid, toss it in, and block it out forever.

No. This gift is a part of me now, as are my daughter and her death. This package is a pledge to myself, but I'll be damned before I put it out of my mind.

So, planting my feet more firmly, I open the lid and I am overcome, washed away, by a wave of relief. The fear and apathy that have been my only companions these past months escape the prison that has become my body and mind. The light filling the room softens and, for the first time in weeks, I hear the harmony of children playing outside. I give myself up to its melody.

Through the window, that before had been void of any life at all, the sky is now so blue, and serene. Watercolor paints have washed over the yard, leaving behind emeralds, diamonds and gold, amethyst, rubies and sapphires to bring life to the garden. All the neighborhood children have gathered in my backyard at the invitation of the play set. The sight of them, running and playing without inhibition, doesn't trouble me, doesn't bring tears to my eyes like it has so often in the past months. I dare to delight in their uncomplicated joy, and the sun brightens even more.

Is it my imagination, or does the box flutter ever so slightly beneath my hands? I hold my breath, waiting for it to happen again. And when it does, I recognize the sensation immediately.

In the box, I see a toddler chasing butterflies and bouncing balls, dancing with kites, shouting to the birds way above her head. A young girl announces that she will someday be one of the clowns doing cartwheels around a circus tent. There she is again, sitting among a group of children, lost in the adventures of Peter Rabbit. Birthday cakes and balloons, music and laughter fill the box. I watch as a mother gently lets go of her daughter, pedaling a bicycle on her own for the first time. A young girl preens in front of a mirror, her mother behind her with a string of pearls for her first dance: a wedding, a young woman gently swinging. I reach out to the infant in her lap and she grasps my finger, and holds so tightly. Her hands are so tiny and porcelain doll perfect. When I brush the light wisp of her dark downy hair away from her eyes, she peers up at me through long silky eyelashes. She smiles and her tiny laugh buries my sorrows. I can see the completeness in her eyes and I know she needs nothing else from this world.

I hear the door creaking slowly, as distracted as the man walking through it. I call out with a hint of hope in my voice, "Come see what we got in the mail today, honey."

He walks through the kitchen doorway, looking through the stack of letters and bills, and probably a card or note with delayed condolences, too. "Did you say something?" he asks without looking up or missing a step toward the end of the kitchen counter, the farthest point from where I now stand, but halfway around the kitchen from the doorway.

"Look, someone sent a gift," hope fading, but my resolve strong. "I don't know who might have sent it, I didn't think I'd missed telling anyone." I felt separated from the voice chattering on and on, and I didn't care if he was listening, so content was I with this gift.

No hello, no how was your day. Instead, he asks the kitchen, "What's in the box?" The twinge of interest in his eyes fades just as quickly, though, when he peers inside. "There's nothing there, is this a joke or something?"

Could it be that he doesn't see what I see, in the box. Or could it be such blatant cruelty that I wouldn't have expected even from him.

Now he stares at me, waiting, expecting an answer I can't give him. There is the familiar blankness in his eyes. No words, just the heaviness in the air. I try to look deep into him, see if there was anything, anything at all there meant for me or our daughter. But, there is nothing.

I pick up the box that has no weight and I walk out of the kitchen. As I cross the threshold of the front door of the house, the sound of my voice is clear and unmistakable, "I did something today."

I wrote this story fourteen years after Katerina's death. It was my memorial to the gifts she had given me; gifts that no one but I could see, gifts that appear seemingly out of nowhere, and feel weightless though they bear all the experiences and events of a lifetime, gifts that restore the will to see the seasons that a full life welcomes.

The release I felt when the story was complete, though, was unexpected, an added bonus. And I realized that moving on was clearly not restricted to dealing with the death alone.

Through the years that had passed, through the attempts at various types of therapy, I was never able to reconcile with the man whose way of coping was to quietly deny the existence of his daughter to himself and everyone around him. When he asked me to deny my own grief, when he refused to let me talk about her to him, or in his presence, I was left to grieve alone.

Fourteen years later, I was no longer alone, and this story helped me realize that I no longer needed to hold on to his betrayal.

* * * * *

I learned that year that people grieve in different ways. But what I couldn't understand, and what was such a tremendous shock to me, was that my husband and I would differ so vastly at how we would come to terms with Katerina's death. After all, we shared her. She was such a strong part of both of us. If we were so far apart on her death, I couldn't at the time even fathom how far apart we'd be in the re-building that needed to take place after.

My husband always had his "walls," and I knew and, at least thought, I understood. When Katerina was born, he was in the Army and in between duty stations. The plan was for me, our three-year old son and the baby to arrive later in the year once he was settled in an apartment. He left for Germany a week after she was born, anxious to get on with his assignment and experience the exhilaration of living in a foreign country. He did not return when she died; duty was his priority and I knew that he would likely grieve alone in much the same way that he loved. Kurt and I were left to the task of closing the shutters on our lives in Topeka, Kansas, covering the furniture so to speak, and making our way five months later to a new home in a different country, and with the different people that we'd become.

We knew from the first day that Katerina's life would be cut dramatically short. The options given to us would only prolong the inevitable. No one could tell me how long she would live, or what her death would be like . . . fast or prolonged, painful or gentle, morning or night, at home or in the car driving down the road. So I tried to make the most of every moment. I slept little, and talked a lot, to whoever would listen. And I tried to maintain myself for Kurt's sake.

I felt that I had only two choices at that point: give in to my grief and shut down as my alter ego in the story had, or put my son first and figure out how to carry on with the day-to-day business of living while I searched for the right place within me for my grief.

My mother-in-law thought I should start attending grief support groups before Katerina died, get a jump on the healing perhaps. I appreciated her intent, but listening to people lament their loss, or describe their shrines, was more than I needed to have to deal with. When it was my turn to talk, I explained my situation. Essentially, my daughter at home and I here were both passing each day knowing that there were a finite number of them. I cried. They told me that I wasn't ready yet to deal with her death; I responded rather tersely that I was more ready than any of them. The experience left me feeling sick and useless and I remember thinking for the first time that death is a release and a test at the same time, that we grieve not for those who have gone but for ourselves and our loss. I went home then to make more memories.

Like I said, people grieve in different ways and I'm in no position to judge how anyone should grieve. Support groups are a wonderful thing. People need to talk . . . whether it's to keep their loved ones memories alive or whether it's to help them process the whole experience . . . we need to talk. And I did, where and when it was comfortable for me, and with people around me who knew and cared about us.

I didn't have a crystal ball, or even my psychic dreams, to tell me what each day would bring. Moving through those long days became tedious. Routine became more important, and not just for my three year old. Being able to say with some certainty that it was time for this action, or at this time we would attend that event, allowed me some degree of control. Katerina and I would take Kurt to pre-school in the morning, and then we'd go somewhere just to be out in the fresh air, the colors of nature, the sounds of happiness, the smells of comfort and love. This was perhaps one of the few gifts that I could give her. We shopped, we ate out, we went to movies, and we relaxed at home just the two of us. But when it was time to pick Kurt up, the three of us would be a family gliding through the evening rituals of dinner, bath, stories, and finally bed.

I felt that I had, in essence, started the grieving process and the moving on process simultaneously.

The day Katerina died was much the same as every other. We got up, got Kurt ready for school and I decided that I would bathe and dress Katerina in a blue dress that brought the morning sky within her reach as soon as we returned. On the way to the school, Kurt chattered and Katerina slept, as she did probably twenty hours a day. But that day she was squeaking . . . that's the only way I can describe the whisper-like sound she made that morning . . . and that was unusual. The teacher asked how we all were that morning; like she did every morning in her own way of expressing anticipation, but all I could muster was a "not so good" though I couldn't have explained why at the time. I rushed out, on the verge of tears from some deep and dark place, and drove straight home. I put a bottle on the stove, I walked slowly around the room, holding Katerina close, talking to her, telling her I loved her, that her brother loved her, that she would be missed, terribly.

Within a half hour I was on the phone, my baby still in my arms, calling the doctor as we'd planned. The nurse insisted that the doctor was not available; I insisted that I needed to talk to her. At an impasse, I finally blurted out that my baby had just died.

The doctor instructed me to go to the funeral home where we were expected. She would meet me there. But if I drove, then I would not be able to keep hold of Katerina. So, I was thankful that my next-door neighbor was home, and agreed to drive us. I wrapped Katerina in a blanket to protect her against the fall chill.

* * * * *

I spent the winter adapting, finding a way to live with my grief, alone. I successfully moved Kurt and I to reunite with my husband and build a home in Germany the following spring. I learned that no matter how hard the challenges I could find a way. I did things. I found a job. I took care of Kurt, and I even tried to start my own survivor's group. I survived the birth of a third child born with congenital heart defects . . . I developed a sense of self that let me decide for myself in what direction I wanted my life, and the life of my children, to go. And I found a comfortable place within me to keep Katerina and her memories, without burdening myself or others.

My husband and I never talked about Katerina. Not even when Kiersten nearly died within minutes of her birth, and the doctors told us that she would not likely survive the flight back to the United States since there was no American pediatric cardiac surgeon in country. Not even after two weeks in a German hospital when she was released, her heart "corrected" but another scar added to my collection. It was like Katerina existed only in my mind.

* * * * *

Fourteen years later, I'm standing in the kitchen of a different house, in a different place, with a different husband and a son and daughter who didn't know their sister, writing a story about the gifts that Katerina gave me. Her short life, and her unfair death, showed me a strength that I had no idea I possessed. And this story reminded me that this strength wasn't limited to her death.

My new husband didn't know us when this all took place. It was years before we met, and so he couldn't possibly have understood what I had experienced. Yet, every year he is with me when I celebrate her birthday and commemorate the date of her death. We talk about her as if we share the memories, we write poems about where or who she would be now, and we throw rose petals into a quiet pond and watch as they float away toward the distant setting sun.

Please note that this is a chapter in a larger project called, *Twenty Years After, A Collection*, that chronicles my process of healing through stories, poems and pictures. My daughter died in 1990 and I have been writing and using photography since we were told she wouldn't live. First to cope, then to remember, and finally to help others who are just embarking on this journey to understand death. I've found nothing else that documents the life-long evolution of healing from the death of a child.

AHEAD OF THE HOPE

MARSHA FISHER
WATERLOO, IOWA

L ittle girls and out-of-body experiences seem slightly incongruous, but my imagination allowed me to soar above the unhappiness of my childhood. One of my earliest memories is of sitting in solitude under one of the huge cedar trees in the back forty of our farm. I suppose it was a form of meditation, although I didn't recognize the word or the process. I was probably about five years old and all I knew was that it gave me solace to be near the roots and trunk of the big tree. As I leaned back and sat, I felt the strength and support I needed to feel grounded and safe. Growing up in Western Washington State, I guess trees are not unlikely nurturing companions, surrounded as I was with towering evergreens and deciduous forests.

Coming from the desolate prairie land of North Dakota in the thirties, my mother thought of Washington as the Garden of Eden and I think I did, too, but for different reasons. A place of green and growing things, it was also a place of foreboding and uncertainty, where the rules of expected behavior by the norms of the fifties, weren't always followed.

I was the youngest of four girls, the child of parents who had migrated from the Midwest following the dryness of the Dust Bowl and the Great Depression. The loss of a farm, harsh immigrant parents, and a shotgun wedding during Hard Times, shaped my own parents to be very hard-working, frugal and goal-oriented. Life had not been easy and continued to be a struggle. Through constant work, usually two jobs, and sacrifice, they managed to own sixty acres of prime farmland in the Nooksack Valley while still in their early forties. However, it didn't come without the price of alcoholism, misunderstandings and strained marital relations. My parents often fought. Verbally vicious and unrelenting, their hard-nosed opposing German and Norwegian roots made for some scary standoffs.

I was born about sixteen years after my oldest sister and we children were really two families. My oldest two sisters were out of the house before I was even aware that they were there. My sister closest in age was not at all pleased to greet me when I finally came home from the hospital. Named after my father, she was to be their last child. The name a concession to the fact he was a German farmer without any sons. Surprisingly, six years later, my mother was pregnant with twins. It was the unknown Rh-negative blood factor that claimed my twin brother's life. The loss of his "blue baby" boy broke my father's heart and his will to work on a marriage and family that had started out of necessity.

It was into this Ibsen-like scenario that I was thrust. Often alone, with no discussion or explanation of the turmoil seething around me, I discovered the fact of my brother's existence in a picture album. I asked who was the little baby in the casket and was told it was my twin brother. I reeled from the realization that I was a twin and that I had had a twin brother who had died. I sought out comfort from the trees. I sorted out my feelings of isolation in the solitude of the cedars. Through the times I'd run to the back forty to think independently under the trees I was given the power to think creatively, compartmentalize the terror of a tenuous family and find inner strength.

Everyday creativity is the ability to see possibilities and see the extraordinary in the ordinary. I continued to grow and started first grade at North Bellingham Elementary School. A little rural school, it often combined two grades in one room. Mrs. Cone was the teacher for both first and second grades; she was old, kind and smelled like expensive face powder. Right after Thanksgiving vacation, we were told she was sick with cancer and she died before Christmas. Her death removed another piece of the stability puzzle that was already missing in parts of my life. Along with the discovery of the death of my twin brother, it consolidated the thought in my head that life was short. My senses seemed to shift into high gear and I looked at each new experience as an exciting chance to reach beyond the sadness of my family and search for an ordering of the universe, or at least an appreciation of it.

I loved art classes and used every chance to illustrate the ideas from books and poetry that we were asked to read or memorize. My high school art teacher doubled as the College English teacher, so his art leaned heavily on the classics. With my research into Greek mythology to develop a wire and multi-media sculpture of "Prometheus Chained", I began to see the immense body of world knowledge available. It helped me realize the need for training and education in the world and past classics to be able to launch into new and creative patterns. I was determined to be the first in my family to attend college.

When my father died of lung cancer in 1962, just after his fiftieth birthday, my creative life philosophy was finished being formulated and confirmed. Life is not only short, but don't get bogged down in the mire of past mistakes as he had; use this problem and think about it as a bridge to a new opportunity. The death of my father was heart wrenching for me. Although he and my mother had a difficult relationship, he tried to reach out to me. I remember asking him to attend a Father-Daughter Banquet for our Campfire Girls' troop. I wanted him to come, but I didn't. I was scared he wouldn't "fit in" and even that he might have a drink before he went and smell like alcohol. I asked him to go and he hugged me and with tears in his eyes, he said, "I don't think I can." I knew the heartache he had of the past had wrenched away his happiness in the future. He did end up going, but I couldn't really enjoy it because I was on pins and needles that he would embarrass me because he was feeling uncomfortable. And I was mad at myself for feeling that way. I thought about this for a long time and realized I needed to be able to see the big picture of the true meaning of life and not perseverate on the small details of the daily grind.

Some of the truisms that I had: "Don't perseverate on the mistakes, but reframe them to be opportunities to learn. Be a future time personality and look ahead with vision. Use the realization that the growth in life is not always linear but organic, as we make connections between similar experiences, possible perspectives and that there is almost always more than one right answer." I had an upcoming opportunity in my life that would put all of this wonderful, creative philosophy to the test.

I met my husband just as I was entering my freshman year at the University of Washington on scholarship. I had worked hard on the vision of attending college and graduated from high school as valedictorian. We dated and were engaged the following spring semester and married in the fall over Thanksgiving weekend. Mike was serving in the Air Force at the time, but when he was discharged in the spring of 1968, we moved back to Mike's hometown of Waterloo, Iowa. He had resumed his job at John Deere and I had completed my teacher training at the University of Northern Iowa. After having two beautiful little girls, Jane and Katie, our life had settled into a pretty complacent routine. Routine, as they say, can breed boredom and questioning of the status quo, as well as a deadening of the senses and the appreciation of the universe that I had worked so hard to achieve as a child.

Soon after, in the fall of 1977, I found out I was pregnant again and we were all delighted! Mike really wanted to have a son to share all his "expertise" in golfing, fishing and hunting and the girls really wanted to have a real baby to play with and I just loved being a mother and couldn't wait to welcome another child into the family. I secretly hoped for a boy too, since I was raised with all girls and my twin brother died soon after birth; I was looking forward to the "Boy Experience".

It was the era of "naturalizing the birth experience" . . . isn't that an oxymoron? Recent medical research was prolific and "profound". Breastfeeding was found to be the healthier alternative to bottles, cigarettes and alcohol were found to be detrimental to the baby in utero, and "natural birth" was being touted as the way to bring your baby into the world. I was adamant about following the healthy guidelines that were recommended and I was considering a natural birth. Since I'd already had two births, it was either very brave or very foolhardy of me. Actually, I had not had natural deliveries for the two girls. Both of them were induced labors, which were fast and furious due to the drug, Pitosen, a drug that immediately threw my body into convulsive labor pains approximately three to four minutes apart at the outset. Their labors were only three and four hours before delivery. Consequently, the idea of a blissful "natural birth" floated in my mind as an angelic alternative. I guess I would vote for my being "foolhardy", as I considered Le Maze as my only anesthetic.

For the first time, my water broke to begin the birth process at home. I was getting out of the bathtub early in the morning, after having pains all night, and I felt that unique flood of water down my legs. We rushed to the hospital and then, waited. The doctor had been in delivery all night and had just gone home for a quick rest. The nurses weren't alarmed after all I was an old hand at this, with two deliveries under my belt. Speaking of belts, they attached an external monitor (it was 1978) and waited. I kept feeling the push and the labor pains, but compared to the forced entries of the girls, they were bearable. I did ask for the doctor repeatedly, but no doctor came until about three hours later. Finally, after the nurses' shift change, an experienced nurse in delivery came in and screamed, "Get her to delivery!" and "Don't push!" to me, as apparently the baby's head had crowned and was fully visible. The "Don't push" was repeated and repeated, until finally the doctor came to catch the baby . . . literally.

It was a boy! He was a beautiful, chubby-checked, eight pound, four ounce boy with fluffy, blond chick-down for hair. Holding him in my arms that bright April morning, while looking out at the puffy, white cloud-filled sky, I prayed thankfully to the gracious God that had given us the son to complete our family. It was a moment that you read about, when your heart physically feels ready to burst with the joy that has filled it. A few moments later, as I was gazing down with rapture at Robert Willard, I saw his little body shiver. Then, I felt the quiver throughout his body and in my mind I had a prosaic "foreshadowing" as I thought to myself, "Something is wrong." I tried to stuff that thought down and simply said to the nurse, "I saw him shiver and felt it, could you check and see if he's okay or if he's cold." The next time I saw Robby, he had a small tube coming out of his nose that was taped to the side of his cheek. He was on a half dose of Phenobarbital to prevent seizures. Gratefully, Robby never suffered from another seizure, but the shadow of dread in the back of my mind cast a pall of concern over the original jubilant joy I had felt. He was only on the medication for a day or so and the general practitioner that we had at the time, Dr. Jones, didn't seem too concerned, since he said he'd had a "difficult delivery". Again, my concern surfaced when the breastfeeding process was so difficult for Robby that the hospital called in a "Le Leche League" nurse. Since I had nursed both of the girls, I'd had some experience, but tried all her suggestions. Nothing seemed to work to get Rob to latch on and suck. I went home with the idea that I'd keep trying, but with little success. The "foreshadow" danced around in the back of my mind.

The next few weeks and then months flew by, with our family adjusting to the cries of the new little one in the house and my trying to accommodate the schedule of a husband, a first-grader, a preschooler and a new baby. I knew that there were some very different behaviors that I was noticing with Robby. He screamed and arched his back when I tried to lay him on his tummy, as the girls had napped. His head always seemed to tilt to the right and he didn't seem to be as attentive to little movements around him as the girls were. I had asked the family doctor at his two-month check-up about his head tilt and he said that he had probably stretched a muscle in his neck during the delivery and not to worry. His lack of muscle tone started to bother me; he couldn't push up with his forearms or hold his head up even a little bit. Finally, it was almost time for his four-month check-up, and I had decided that if Dr. Jones didn't recommend seeing a pediatrician, I was going to ask for a referral. The "shadow" was starting to become a menacing figure that was haunting my daily thoughts.

The day had arrived and when I went into the doctor's examination room, I had rehearsed my reasons and readied my request for a second opinion. Dr. Jones came in and in a few minutes explained that he had requested a neurological pediatrician to come in for the appointment also to check Robby over. Dr. LePoidivin, a chic, sophisticated woman came in brusquely and gave Robby the "once over". She pronounced that he had "neurological difficulties" causing his delays. Something clicked in the back of my mind and the furtive shadow seemed to be nodding. After the appointment, I hurried home with the baby and when my other motherly duties were fulfilled, I rushed down to the basement and dug into my boxes of college textbooks. The term, "neurological difficulties and delays" was like a lyric from a song that I couldn't think of the name. Flipping through the index of a child development book, I found the pages to describe what exactly the medical term meant. It was loosely connected to "cerebral palsy". That afternoon, I called my husband, Mike and told him what the doctor had said and what I had found. I said, "With God's help, we can do this. I love you."

I cried and cried and then realized with remorse, the sadness my parents must have felt with the death of my twin brother. Of course, Robby wasn't dead. He was healthy in all other ways besides the neuromuscular connections in his brain. What was dead were the typical dreams that parents hold for their children. The third pregnancy could be described as a trip into familiar territory, one that you have explored before and had some expectations of the lay of the land. Yep, we were jetting off to Minneapolis, but somehow we landed in Miami. All reservations for the golf courses, the ball diamonds, and target shooting were canceled. Unknown reservations were being made without our knowledge or understanding. It was a difficult time.

Creativity is a matter of perspective. I remember returning to my mom's bowling league for the first time after Rob's diagnosis and as I rolled the same ball down the same lane with the same girls as before, I was thinking, "My life will never be the same. It won't necessarily be bad, but it will be different." I was determined to look to the future with hope and to do that I would have to employ the creative philosophy and truisms I had developed to deal with my childhood. I knew I needed to use a new paradigm to break the pattern of regret and depression that had enveloped my parents' lives.

Take time to meditate. I knew I would need to take some time for myself and develop the inner strength that guided me through my childhood. Although I now lived in the Midwest and couldn't run to the back forty and sit under a huge cedar tree, I found I had to find alone time to think and build a reserve of inner strength. Sometimes, it was three in the morning while folding clothes or falling asleep in the bathtub with a locked door.

Compartmentalize to break the pattern of sorrow. The fact was that Rob would not develop physically or mentally in the same way as our other children, but he could still be loved and love us. He would provide us and our other children with the bridge to many new opportunities to learn. All of our children—we later had a son, Joe, four years younger than Rob—are in service professions: Ultrasonography, School District Administrator, and Police Officer. The compassion and understanding of people with different abilities and backgrounds was expanded through our experiences with Rob. I have followed a career in teaching that began before Rob that has been enriched by him. It now has included working with diverse populations, including children of generational poverty and special needs, as well as teaching college students strategies to use to be successful in teaching all students.

Look to the future with vision. What did we hope for Robby in five years? In ten years? In twenty? As I was planning from childhood to increase my knowledge of the world outside my home and to go to college, Steven Covey's mantra of "Begin with the end in mind" is a guide to harnessing creative, out-of-the-box thinking to original ideas that have value. Where did we see Rob living as an adult? What did we hope for him in his life? During his early life, we knew we wanted him to be a part of our family. We were not ready to send him off to a "residential facility" as was suggested by some. We fought to have him attend a special preschool. The agency said they didn't have van transportation, so we provided it. Later, we knew we wanted him to live in a typical community in his future and not be in an institution, so we advocated for him to be included in typical public school classes. This was for him to learn appropriate social skills, but to also help typical children learn the wonderful personality that was our son, Rob. This has proven to be a great decision, with high school classmates greeting him heartily at his ten-year class reunion and a middle school friend remembering him and inviting him to his wedding.

Rob was in elementary school in the eighties, when the idea of full inclusion for special needs students was gaining popularity. He had a fantastic elementary special needs teacher, Ruth Riehle, who knew children were more accepting than adults and worked to emphasize the similarities or likenesses of all of us, that is our emotional and social needs, rather than our physical or mental differences. As Rob entered middle school in the early nineties, I knew that full inclusion was not going to give him the time and instruction he needed, so we opted for smaller classes for students with learning disabilities. Today, the idea of individualized and customized educational services for each student is the norm and more appropriate. Seeing the possibilities through adaptation of the ordinary made an extraordinary, valued and creative life for Rob.

Life and learning grows organically and collaboratively. My parents' individual isolation and avoidance of the discussion of their feelings and pain provided an unhealthy mix in which to grow. When I called Mike, my husband, I said, "we" could face this together with God. We have worked through the stress and strain of a son with quadriplegic cerebral palsy together. It hasn't been a lovely, linear road to happiness. We have had loud and defiant discussions. We have had sobbing with sad and tear-filled emotions. We have fought. But, we have come together for the common good of Rob and for our family. We have spurts of growth and then steps backward, but we are working on our relationship and for our family, together.

Reaching out for the support of other families and professionals was an early survival activity for us. I saw a lady with a young boy in a wheelchair at a swimming pool before Rob was diagnosed. She was bringing her daughter to lessons, just as I was bringing the girls to swim lessons, too. When I saw her at Kmart following the confirmation of my suspicions of Rob's cerebral palsy, I went up and asked her "how she did it", meaning taking care of a disabled young child and other children. Her frank, honest and supportive suggestions were of help to me during those early stages of adjustment and we have tried to help other young families through our involvement with "Up With Families" and other support groups. Even today, I find networking through a "Margarita Club" of women with "differently abled" children, many now young adults and learn of resources and programs for adults with disabilities. Collaboration increases creativity as "many hands lighten the load" and many perspectives bring new ideas.

Asking intuitive questions of the medical professionals and establishment has helped both our family and the professionals to grow. We often encourage the professionals to think of their human side as they begin to view their "client", i.e., Rob from a personalized model instead of a medical model. While at University of Iowa Children's hospital for multiple checkups and reaching no definitive answers, we once asked a doctor, "What would you do if this was your child?" He honestly replied, "I'd ask for a second opinion." He even suggested two world-class hospitals that we could try. Thank God for his humanity and personal approach. When we took Rob to Gillette Regional Hospital for Children with Disabilities, we were immediately scheduled for a necessary surgery. Without their knowledge and understanding of the foreseeable future through their longitudinal studies, Rob would have been forced into nursing care as a 165-pound adult, since he would not have been able to stand to transfer due to foot drop.

Today, Rob has reached out to the world himself for friendship and support. He is thirty-four years old and has a very social and caring nature. He sees the world as a warm and receptive place and in most cases, believes in the good of people. Through a Sirius radio program, "The Paul Finebaum Show", Rob has become a regular caller and radio personality, "Robert from Waterloo". At least in the area of the SEC, the southeastern sports conference, he has become synonymous with someone who enjoys sports, loves talking with different types of people and who has overcome some of life's adversities. His popularity among the radio audience was not only surprising but a phenomenon that is inspirational. After about a year and a half of being a regular on the show, in the fall of 2011, Paul and an entourage of "his people" flew up to Waterloo one morning to visit Rob and take us out to lunch, returning by private jet to do his afternoon show. Last fall, (2012) we traveled to Alabama to visit all of Rob's radio friends, staying with Jimbo Parsons and his family in Birmingham. The graciousness of the South was reinforced by the wonderful hospitality and kindness we received. Rob's voice was recognized in restaurants and gas stations, drawing a crowd of people and admirers. The visit to the Quad at the University of Alabama was unbelievable as fans stopped his wheelchair every few feet for a picture and autograph. The creative vision of himself as a contributing adult with connections to the typical world has come true through the collaboration of caring people and his family, including a mother who was a girl from a small farm in Washington.

Creativity allowed this young girl with a woeful home life to learn to find peace and inner strength through meditation. It gave her the process of compartmentalizing, to accept the facts and move on and not to get stuck in a pattern of misery. To have her realize that problems can be reframed through a different perspective to be a bridge to new, wider and richer opportunities of learning about the world. And to reach out to communicate with the people and resources around her to build and grow in the grace-filled life she was given. With creativity, life's bumps can be seen as launching pads to worlds and experiences that you might never have been able to experience. So ahead of the hope for a perfect life, must come creativity to take life as it is and make it hopeful.

FIFTH PLACE WINNER

MOURNING PAGES

LESLEY PEARL
CHICAGO, IL

"**I** am alone because I am getting ready to be alone."
Every day the same words spilled out of my pen and onto my notebook. It was March. I was staying at a friend's house in Northern California, while she and her partner were in Hawaii. In their week long absence, they left me their home, a car and a neurotic dog named Zach.

Every morning was the same.

I'd mash a banana into a bowl; cover it with dry oats and water and microwave for three minutes—adding blueberries and soymilk after cooking. French press a pot of coffee. Open the sliding glass door for Zack to go outside. Sit at the table next to fireplace and write three pages, longhand.

I was in Week 4 of Julia Cameron's, *The Artist's Way: A Spiritual Path to Higher Creativity*.

The book had been suggested to me for nearly eighteen years, but I had only recently picked it up. Pain is a great motivator. So is time.

I was living in Seattle. I'd been there just a little more than six months. It was my second cross-country move in less than five years. The first, to Chicago from San Francisco, for my husband's medical residency. The second, to Seattle, for his dream job.

Both times, I closed up my massage practice. Handed over my Weight Watchers meetings to another leader. Threw a send-off soiree, and said a tearful goodbye to my friends. Following in his path. Next time would be my turn. That was the promise we made.

I wasn't working much. I didn't have a massage license. I was clinically depressed. My husband encouraged me to take it easy. He reminded me that his job as a doctor, and the six-figure salary that went along with it—that it was for us. That this is what he had been working for. That now I could breathe and think about what "my turn" might look like.

I hadn't a clue.

Rabbinical school? Acupuncture school? Nothing seemed certain.

Devoid of any clear sense of direction, I picked up the book that had been recommended to me so many times over the years.

I dug in with a hunger and willingness I hadn't known since getting sober nearly five years earlier. I read each page carefully, highlighter in hand, taking notes in the margins. Looking for a clue. For a promise of direction. Or at the very least, something meaningful to do with my time.

Each week had a title. "Recovering a Sense of . . ."—fill in the blank. It included readings, suggested exercises, and questions for reflection at week's end. Two constants ran through the entire twelve weeks, what Cameron calls the primary tools of creative recovery—Morning Pages and the Artist Date.

Morning Pages were simply that—three pages written longhand, first thing in the morning. Before diving into email. Before opening up the newspaper. Before dressing children. Cleaning the house. Talking to the nanny. Making dinner plans. Before Pilates.

Morning pages were not meant to be art. Or for anyone to even read. They were a practice. "Spilling out of bed and straight onto the page." Without expectations. Without judgment. Simply making room for new input. Morning pages, she said, were non-negotiable.

An Artist Date was a kind of fancy, little-bit grown up, name for a play date—alone. No friends. No spouses. No children. A block of time for spoiling and nurturing oneself—creatively.

* * * * *

The tools gave my life structure. Something to hang my day on. I would wake early each morning, before my husband, make oatmeal with blueberries and banana, coffee, turn on my light box and write.

The routine was established by the time I arrived in California in March. I found it easy to recreate my process in this new, albeit temporary, space.

I had begun to notice patterns emerging in my morning pages. The same themes popping up like whack-a-moles again and again. But I didn't have to race to pound them down with a big, padded mallet. I could let them sit on the page. Powerless.

So I wasn't exactly surprised when I wrote, "I am alone because I am getting ready to be alone." I knew exactly what it meant. And I wasn't afraid.

* * * * *

We had been struggling for a while. Pretty much since we arrived in Chicago nearly five years earlier. He started medical residency. I quit drinking. Our lives took radically divergent paths. And like a vector, kept moving further in opposite directions.

Nine days before we left Chicago, he told me I didn't have to go to Seattle. He didn't want to be the guy who once again took me from my home, my friends and my livelihood. I was shocked. Stuck. I couldn't turn around that fast, even if I had wanted to. Besides, we had already rented out our condominium. I'd given up my office and my work.

We moved forward—together—as planned. We hosted a going-away party that weekend—assuming our roles in the story of us as happy couple. And a few days later, we were gone.

Within weeks of arriving in Seattle, my husband asked me for a divorce. The next day he retracted his request and admitted he might be acting hastily. We agreed to see a couple's counselor. A smart, young woman, many years our junior, who asked, "How will you know?" Meaning, how would we know when it was time to call it quits.

Neither of us could answer. I meditated on the question all week. The words came to me in the stillness of waiting.

"You know what not working on your marriage looks like. Why don't you see what working on your marriage looks like?"

I instantly felt a shift in my body—as if I had just experienced a chiropractic adjustment. I had an immediate sense of ease. An increase in energy and flow. I knew it was right. I told my husband, and together we told our therapist that we had decided "not to decide," for six months. Instead, choosing to focus our energies on the work.

It was during that six-month period that I went back to California, stayed in the big house with the fireplace and the neurotic dog, and wrote the same words each day. I shared them with no one.

* * * * *

My husband flew down to join me at the end of the week. Before picking him up, I met with a local Rabbi. He replaced the one I had studied with many years earlier, before I was married. He had died unexpectedly. His passing was a source of remorse and pain, mostly as we had never completed our studies. I had slipped away without a word. Just about the time I met my husband.

I told the replacement Rabbi that I might want to be a Rabbi. But that I couldn't see how to do it, to stay married, and continue to work on my marriage. He said if it was my path, it would find me.

My husband and I greeted one another at San Francisco International Airport, irritated, obligated. I remembered coming home from a trip, not long after meeting him. He met me at the gate, flowers in hand. I literally ran to him and jumped into his arms, wrapping my legs around his waist. We were no longer that couple. And we hadn't been for a long time.

I drove us back to the big house with the glass fireplace and the neurotic dog. I told him about the flood of memories that I had experienced that week. That they had nearly drowned me. That everywhere I turned, I was reminded of us. Especially of the hours we spent together on our bikes.

"It got too hard," he said. "I didn't want to do it anymore."

"Ride with me?" I asked, referring to the chasm between our cycling abilities—a regular source of tension between us. "Or be married?"

"Both."

And there it was—the truth that I had written every morning. The truth that I knew because I did write every morning. The truth that I had known in my bones before he ever arrived.

I wish I could say I was calm. That I stood in awe of my knowing. In awe of the serendipity. That the truth was spoken in the city where lived together for nearly 10 years, in the neighborhood where we met. But I wasn't. My wheels rolled on to the Golden Gate Bridge. I thought about driving off. Instead, I yelled. A lot.

I was in the middle of Week Four in *The Artist's Way*—Recovering a Sense of Integrity.

* * * * *

Returning home to Seattle, I named *The Artist's Way* my companion in divorce. It seemed the only thing I knew to do. That, and walk. Miles and miles with no particular destination. The heels of my tan suede boots were re-soled during this time.

I continued to write. To look for synchronicity in my life, as I was directed in the book. Truthfully, I couldn't imagine any greater synchronicity than what I had just experienced.

I went on occasional Artist Dates but couldn't fully commit to the practice.

I bought The Writer's Market and considered writing again professionally.

I made Benjamin Franklin T-squares, lists of pro and con, trying to determine where I should call home. Seattle? Chicago? San Francisco?

I sent *The Artist's Way* to my friend in Chicago who was also going through a divorce.

I told him it was a book of miracles, my trusted companion during this time of transition. I told him about my morning pages. About being in that house alone and knowing that I was preparing to be alone.

I told him about the Rabbi who said if rabbinical school was my path, that it would find me. And that my husband asking for a divorce felt like being found. That I had become open to these messages because of the book. And because of the creative work I had done.

I finished the twelve weeks of *The Artist's Way*.

And then I went to Rwanda.

I had planned the trip several weeks earlier. I would be traveling with members of my synagogue—touring, witnessing and working with two different AIDS organizations. It was there, under my mosquito net in sub-Saharan Africa, that I heard the next creative whisper, received my next set of instructions.

I started blogging.

* * * * *

I entered university nearly 25 years prior, majoring in fine art. I graduated with a degree in journalism—my parents insisting I choose a more practical focus.

I spent the next five years toiling at a series of weekly newspapers, and then left the profession entirely. I wanted to make more money. Which I did. I wanted to tell my stories, instead of someone else's. Which I didn't—unless you count drunken scrawls in journals and poems stuffed under the bed.

In Africa, I wrote each night before bed. After my roommate and I finished debriefing about our days. When the sky was navy and the air was still with silence—nothingness. I wrote by the light of the computer screen.

I described the land, its people and my experiences with both in lush detail. The smell of oranges mixed with diesel. Churches where bloodied clothes remained, remnants of the most recent genocide. Children born with HIV acting as mentors to those younger than themselves, also born with the disease.

The houses made of mud brick. A calendar on the wall—a single decoration. The woman who built her own house, and then another which she rents. Who sells charcoal, and can now care for herself and her children—mostly. Women and children robed in colorful fabrics, walking on the side of the road—24 hours a day, fruit or furniture balanced on their heads.

Reed thin men pushing bicycles weighted down with four or six yellow jerry cans of water. An opening gala at an art co-operative tucked into a downtrodden neighborhood. Peeing ridiculously close to a giraffe while on safari.

I posted my blogs to Facebook in the wee hours when I could get an internet signal. Following each posting I was greeted with words from the unlikeliest of Facebook "friends." Girls I went to Adat Shalom nursery school with in the early 1970s, friends' husbands I hardly knew, and associates of my Rabbi. They all said the same thing. "Thank you." And "Keep writing."

But I didn't. Not for three months. I didn't write about my divorce. My drive cross country. My first time living alone in 43 years. I didn't write a word—until I received a call that my birthmother was dying. A woman I had met only three years prior, who at 59, was dying.

I flew out of Chicago the next day, pacing just in front of Hurricane Sandy. When I arrived she was hooked up to IVs and monitors, barely 100 pounds in a hospital gown. There was nowhere for her to hide anymore. She could no longer act the part she thought I wanted her to be. We were both stripped down and naked. And I felt, perhaps for the first time, nothing but love for her.

I played Pandora radio for her. Danced and held her hand to "Love Train" by the O Jays. I massaged her feet, her papery skin. I sobbed on her bed. And I found healing.

I told her about a man I met there in South Carolina. How he swept me off my feet —literally picking me up off of the ground the first time I met him. And how he broke my heart a few days later—slipping away without a word.

I chronicled all of it, blogging. My inbox filled with personal notes. Words of encouragement. Stories shared. From former co-workers. Friends of my birthmother. Cousins I had never met. Even the man from South Carolina who broke my heart.

I felt seen. Connected. The connection I had craved all of my life. That I had twisted myself inside and out for. Here it was. And all I had to do to receive it was to tell my truth. To write it. And to share it—publicly.

So I did.

I wrote about living alone. About throwing out food because I didn't know how to shop for one anymore. About my Jewish divorce—my

Get . . . And my civil divorce. About my breast reduction—a surgery so fraught with pain and shame I had barely spoken of it.

And then, about my second time through *The Artist's Way.*

* * * * *

I didn't date after my ex-husband asked me for a divorce. I experienced intimate friendships—hours spent on the phone telling one another every detail about ourselves. Sexy kisses under the moon that made me feel like I was seventeen. Over the top expectations and the crash that accompanied them. But I had not dated.

I wasn't ready. I was too vulnerable. But I was lonely. So I took on *The Artist's Way* again as my companion, this time committing myself to the Artist Dates. Those two-or-so hour play dates by myself.

I perused gourmet food shops. Spent hours at a bookstore, tucked in a chair with an Annie Leibowitz anthology in my lap. I bought myself little trinkets and had them giftwrapped.

I went to the movies. Walked on the beach in winter. And at the bird and butterfly sanctuary. I scoured thrift stores. Visited the polar bear at the Lincoln Park Zoo.

I went to the art supply store. And to the Art Institute—many times. Visiting Marc Chagall's America Windows again and again. I went to the Lebanese and Indian neighborhoods. Ate syrupy sweet desserts and shopped with women wearing saris and chadors. I popped into interesting boutiques I'd eyed and wondered about, but had never stepped foot in.

I went to the Joffrey Ballet.

All of it, alone. And then I chronicled each experience.

I wrote about my ex-husband sending me boxes of things I left behind, and not wanting to open them. About being afraid of Week 4 in *The Artist's Way* because that was the week my ex asked me for a divorce.

I wrote about how strange and uncomfortable it was when my father asked me if I was dating. How uncomfortable he was when I said no, and how I felt the need to explain my decision to him. How I told him that I had work to do.

I let go of work I no longer enjoyed, and leaned heavily into my spousal support.

I took dance classes—Mambo and West African. I attended performances and lectures—on my own and with girlfriends. I began cooking again. Collaging. And I kept writing. Blogging.

The Artist Dates had become a habit. I enjoyed a $6 piece of torte and coffee served on a silver tray on a Friday afternoon, just because. I brought home a silk kimono from Japan and an embroidered, well-loved bedspread from the thrift store, just because they were beautiful.

I began to treat myself as well, if not better, than anyone else had ever treated me.

I began to turn inward, to lean into my pain. The hurt of love ending. Of promises broken. The fear of a big, empty canvas of life. I gave it a name and a face—with words, and with paintbrushes, pencils and pretty paper, with movement. And I found it wasn't quite so scary when I did.

I found my voice. The one that wrote, "I am alone because I am getting ready to be alone," continuing to spill out of me every morning and onto three blank pages. Mourning pages.

THE MIRACLES OF LIFE, MODERN MEDICINE, AND ANCIENT HEALING

LAURA BROWN
PARKDALE, OR

I t all started on the beautiful Northern Island of New Zealand. Hawkes Bay, Napier, to be exact. We were on a "working holiday" with my husband's work. Scott had been hired on for at least one year, longer if we wanted to stay and all worked out. My husband Scott, Lienne who was two at the time, and I had been living in New Zealand for nearly a year when Silas was conceived. We were so excited to be pregnant again, as we really wanted two children all along. We had decided we wanted to stay longer, all was working out, and we loved New Zealand. My brother, Erik, was soon to be married back in the States. So we purchased round trip tickets to the San Francisco airport to attend my brother's wedding in the Sacramento area, with the plan of returning to New Zealand.

Something changed. We started coming up against big roadblocks. The timing, our visa process, and my strong feelings of feeling like we should go "home" started to take control. It eventually became clear that we would not be able to work out our visa issues in time, and we would not be able to return to New Zealand as planned. So we changed our round trip tickets to 'one-way' and took a financial "ding", but this was what we were being guided to do.

We returned to the United States in October of 2009. My pregnancy was going smoothly and beautifully, even though I was experiencing nausea by this time. "Just a sign of a good healthy baby in there," we all agreed. My sister-in-law, Kelly, was joyfully pregnant at the same time. We were all so excited to be going through this process together, and to know our children would be growing up together.

We decided to return to Humboldt County, California, where Scott and I had originally met during our college days. I had been experiencing very strong feelings about returning to our old "stomping ground", even though it really did not make sense in a lot of ways. I felt I could no longer ignore the strong feelings, so my husband was on board as well . . . well at least he said, "Yes Dear." Later we learned from our local clairvoyant woman in Arcata, that it was indeed Silas, who felt that he needed to be born back in Humboldt County, as we had a strong support group there, and we all needed it.

The medical insurance journey was a long challenging road, but all turned for the absolute best. Insurance companies were not willing to insure us, as I had a "pre-existing condition"; I was already pregnant. Wow. Also not to mention, being away from the States for a year. So, family and friends encouraged me to explore Medi-Cal (Medicaid program in the State of California). I was determined to continue, "jumping through the hoops" to receive coverage for this pregnancy and delivery. Sure enough by my eighth month of pregnancy, thankfully they accepted us. Who knew they would be saving us from financial breakdown, as our medical bills were going to be well over a million dollars.

We considered a homebirth again, as we considered with our first child. I really wanted to experience a home and water birth, what a natural beautiful way to bring a new Being into the world. However, there was something inside both my husband and myself that advised us against a home birth this time around. Not to mention, Medi-Cal would not cover a homebirth. My routine visits to my clinic of choice, all checked out well and healthy. Baby Brown was growing beautifully with a strong healthy heartbeat. I felt very grateful for the clinic I chose, as there were midwives on board, and I was legally allowed to labor and deliver in the water at the local hospital's birthing center.

Our baby boy was nearing his due date. We had a lovely doula on board, a birth plan that requested the birth to be "all natural", and a birthing tub reserved and ready to go. My labor progressed comfortably and steadily over a span of a few days. My mom had arrived a couple of days before I started laboring. My water broke the morning of May 23, 2010. I waited as long as possible before going to the birthing center. It was a beautiful sunny day, and I had a beautiful neighborhood to walk around to get things moving. I had bought Lienne a new bathing suit so she could get into the tub with me. As well as a "fairy" outfit to wear as soon as her baby brother was born, signifying her entry into "Big Sister Role."

We arrived at the hospital birthing center in the late afternoon. The midwife on duty suggested I may be further along than I thought, and to come in to get checked out to see how I was progressing. My labor felt so comfortable, I even chose to be the driver of the car to the birthing center. When I arrived and appeared to be so comfortable and calm, the nurses replied, "You would be in a lot more pain and discomfort if you were very far along, but let's go ahead and check your progress anyway, since you're here." So sure enough, I was extremely dilated, and contractions were very real indeed. They said, "You are going to have this baby very soon, we will get you into a delivery room right away." I continued to walk around the beautiful outdoor premises of the hospital and could feel his head coming down, so I returned back to my room to get into the tub. I continued laboring in the tub for about an hour.

Everything was progressing so beautifully and comfortably, until it was time to push. It became very painful and uncomfortable pretty quickly. I started singing and chanting very loudly. We were all surprised at the Native American sounds coming from me. I had never heard myself sound like this before. It felt like something or someone else was coming through me. My husband was surprised, as he had never heard me sound like this either.

After a few pushes, my midwife told me we needed to "get out of the water, baby is not doing well." Still unworried at the time, I was disappointed I had to get out of the water to finish pushing him out on a hospital bed. I again found myself flat on my back, my least favorite position to be in for contractions and pushing. My midwife began to sound firm. I remember hearing her say, "We need to get this baby out right away." She stayed calm and professional the entire time. She was brilliant, we could not have asked for a more perfect person to deliver our incredible baby. By this time, she knew something was wrong. I was pushing as hard as I could, and he would not budge. His shoulder was stuck. So the midwife climbed onto the bed with me, and reached in and pulled him out. She had already called for the emergency team with oxygen and resuscitation equipment, to come to the delivery room, so they were standing by. They took him away as soon as he came out, no contact whatsoever, and started resuscitation efforts on him immediately, just a few feet away from me.

"How come he's not crying yet?" I said to my husband as the emergency team was working on him.

"I don't know," he responded. They eventually rolled him completely out of the room. My husband followed our brand new baby boy, knowing I had a whole medical and emotional support team at my side. Scott was at Silas's side the entire time, touching him and talking to him. Talk about immediate father and son bonding, truly very special. Little did we know at that point, we would soon have to go through an extended period of time, having no physical contact with Silas.

Next, I remember the midwife saying, "This is one of those circumstances where your baby needed to be taken away for more support." I was numb, I don't remember feeling any emotion at that point. I guess I was in denial, thinking he would be fine, and would be back in my arms to nurse in just a few minutes. She then proceeded to tell me I was torn so badly they needed to call in a topnotch surgeon to sew me up, as it was too extensive for her to stich herself. While I was waiting for the surgeon to arrive, I still did not know what was happening with my baby.

I remember a couple of nurses telling me the surgeon that was coming to sew me up was incredible, and I would be very happy with his work. Well great, that's something to look forward to, I thought. Come to find out later, the surgeon also said to my husband, "You'll be very pleased with my work."

As I was being sewn up by this "magical women's doctor", which ended up being a two hour procedure, a local pediatrician came into my room. He informed me our son was born with a Congenital Diaphragmatic Hernia (CDH). Which means he had a hole in his diaphragm, and his intestines had migrated up into his chest cavity, crushing his lungs. He said he needed to be airlifted to a major hospital, and recommended UCSF San Francisco Children's Hospital almost 300 miles away, as they had one of the top teams in the nation for this birth defect. He also informed me he would be there for a while, as he had a good amount of experience with babies born with CDH.

I was in shock . . . completely stunned. I was not even really crying yet, and felt horrible that I wasn't. What's wrong with me? I thought. I remember "negotiating" a bit with the pediatrician asking about Seattle, WA, as I had family there, and we could stay with them for a while. He really emphasized that this was a very serious case, and encouraged me to go with San Francisco Children's Hospital. He just needed our consent to make the telephone call to get the flight team moving. Ok, things were starting to sink in now. My husband was still with our new baby boy, Silas Anthony Brown. My mom was at my side the entire time, as well as others coming and going trying to keep me in the loop.

I requested someone to help Lienne get dressed into her 'Big Sister Fairy Outfit.' As crushing and absolutely devastating as this experience was, Lienne still had a baby brother, and was officially a big sister now. I was finally vaginally sewn back together, and was now able to be wheeled in to see my son. Words cannot explain how devastating it was to see him at that point. It was the beginning of the saddest experience of my life. All I wanted to do was pick him up, hold him, and nurse him. He was in an oxygen hood and heavily medicated. We could only touch part of his body and talk to him. We waited by his side for the San Francisco Children's Intensive Care Flight Team to come get him and take him away.

Take him away? Is this really happening? I remember thinking. We were just at this birthing center a few weeks prior getting a tour for our upcoming delivery. They showed us the room where babies are taken when they cannot be with their mother. I remember feeling and thinking, how sad for those families. I also remember hearing a baby's non-stop crying in "the room", and our tour guide said, "That baby wants its mama." It hurt my heart even then. It was nearing one o'clock in the morning, and Lienne was asleep in our overnight room, as she would continue to be with us the entire time.

I remember feeling exhaustion and blood soaking through everything, as I had to stand to touch Silas. I just wanted to lie down and nurse my new baby boy peacefully. The flight team had arrived. What a long and meticulous process they went through to stabilize him for the flight. They were all so nice and as comforting as could be. They did not have any answers for us. They were just there to take our precious baby to the care he needed. It was a shock to learn we could not fly with him. I just assumed at least one of us would be able to fly with him. We had to say our heart-breaking "goodbyes" to our brand new baby. Hardest thing ever, hands down.

It was time for us to go to our room now to sleep. Sleep? How? It would be daylight soon; we had a three-year-old daughter to take care of, and a lot of work to get us down to San Francisco. I started pumping upon entering our overnight room. Saving every little drop of colostrum I could muster. I was determined to get my colostrum and milk to Silas. From that point on, I would be pumping every two to three hours around the clock. First thing Lienne said when she woke up, "Where is Silas?" Tears just kept streaming and I could not even answer her. Thankfully, Scott was able to speak. Now we were just waiting for the check out process. There was one Labor and Delivery team member who came in to give us a hospital baby t-shirt and give us the "low down" on some check out items. I could not stop crying. We were not going home with our baby. Did he not get the message? Our midwife also came in for a morning visit. She was very positive. She told us she believes it is families like ours that come through these situations successfully. It helped for sure. I had many years experience working with children who had a variety of developmental disabilities, and I thought, you're right, we can do this. Maybe this is why I spent so many years working with the special needs population.

We were finally released later that afternoon. I called my mom on the drive to let her know we were coming home, as she had slept at our house. What a different phone call than with our firstborn, when we were excited to say we were coming home with our newborn baby. It felt so empty and depressing to be driving home with an empty car seat in the back next to Lienne. We arrived home to neighbors, friends, and my mother's undying support. How ever will we get packed and ready for a five-hour road trip to go be with our new baby?

Erik, my brother, had been involved from a distance from the moment Silas was born. He had been woken up to a telephone call from my mom who could not stop crying enough to explain what was happening. Erik had to ask, "Is Laura alive?"

She was able to say, "Yes."

He then asked, "Is the baby alive?"

She wept, "Yes, but he can't breath on his own." Erik had purchased the soonest airline ticket he could, to fly down from Seattle, to be with Silas while we were getting it together to drive down.

"He's a newborn. He needs as much human touch as we can give him, and I can get on the next flight." he said. So off he went, leaving his new five week old baby boy, Kody and wife, Kelly, to be with Silas who needed a family member at his side. Later, they would all return together, making a seventeen-hour drive from Seattle, continuing their amazing support for us.

Our drive finally began the next day. Another twenty-four hours had gone by before we could see our precious new baby. What a long and quiet trip down to San Francisco. I continued to pump my milk in the car on the way. When we arrived at San Francisco Children's Hospital we had family waiting for us in the waiting room. It was so comforting. What mixed feelings I had seeing Silas again. I was excited to see our new baby, wanting to look him over again, what color are his eyes? What color is his hair? What does his face look like? Wow, it seemed like there was every kind of machine hooked up to him. He was now intubated and on a ventilator. We were no longer allowed to touch him, as it would be too stimulating for him. Uncle Erik was able to lay his hand upon the top of his head (the only place without tubes, pads, or sensors) off and on throughout the first two days. They were working on stabilizing him for surgery. They had no idea how long this would take, and if he would even be able to have surgery. They had him in a chemically induced coma to keep him from being stimulated. Little did we know it would be a long time before we would see him with his eyes open.

Later, we learned how critical Silas's first few days were. My brother Erik was a Seattle firefighter and his wife Kelly was an ICU nurse at the trauma center in Seattle. As it turned out, one of Kelly's co-workers was the sister of one of Silas's nurses. Because of the bond they shared, more 'sensitive' information about Silas's condition was shared with Erik. One of the flight team nurses that picked Silas up expressed that she believed our midwife played a most critical role in Silas surviving the delivery with her swift and competent action during a double complication (unexpected CDH and shoulder dystocia—a stuck shoulder). She also shared that Silas had to be resuscitated several times during the transport, and he was given only a twenty percent chance of survival upon arrival at San Francisco's Children's Hospital. However, no one, including Erik, told us this information until much later, thankfully. On a positive note, Silas was born at full term, eight pounds, one ounce, and his liver was not involved, which was a big plus for these babies.

It took five days to stabilize him enough for surgery. This felt like our "last hope." We were given best and worst case scenarios. We were told the best case was a "late" onset hernia with a small hole. This would mean his diaphragm tore later during the pregnancy after his lungs were developed and the hole could be repaired with just sutures. In this case, they would simply pull his intestines out of his chest making room for his lungs to fully inflate, sew up the hole, and Silas would more than likely have a "normal" life. Worst case we were told was an "early" onset tear, which would mean the hole was probably larger, thus needing a patch, and his lungs would not have had the room to fully develop. The majority of these babies go home with a feeding tube and oxygen for at least the first year of life, and need the patch replaced between age two and four. This would be a very "long road" to recovery just to survive, and had a poor prognosis for a "normal" life.

I remember asking every question I could think of hoping the team of doctors would have a guess of what we were up against. They informed us it was very rare not to be discovered during my pregnancy. They optimistically thought this could be a sign that the hernia was a "late" onset, meaning the hole could be small. We were holding onto this hope as well. Normally these deliveries are done right at

UCSF Hospital, so the team is ready for the baby immediately. As most babies who are born with CDH away from an experienced team, do not survive. In fact, these babies just recently started surviving. They informed us numerous times how fortunate we were to have the team we did in Arcata. As the pediatrician and midwife knew exactly what to do, which can be very rare in such a small area. A couple of my friends back in New Zealand expressed their happiness for us that he was born in the States, as they truly felt New Zealand was not equipped to handle this advanced of a case. I am so thankful for the guidance that led us back to the States.

I was definitely on a roller coaster of emotions in so many ways, not to mention just being "hormonal" after giving birth. What did I do wrong? Was it really my fault? Why us? Is this really just a bad dream? It was my fault, how could I let him down? If only . . . Maybe it was all of the stress at the beginning of my pregnancy. Was it the spray on tan I had done for the wedding? Or all the hairspray they used on my hair for the wedding? What happened? I remember the lovely Social Worker at the hospital looking straight into my eyes one day, as if she could read my mind, "You know this is not your fault right? This is not your fault. This is not your fault . . ." She continued to repeat this until I cried.

Surgery day was my lowest point. We waited and waited while he was in surgery, it seemed to be taking so long. At one point, they informed us he was doing great and it was going very well. How exciting! This was it; it's just a small hole, I thought. Until the doctor came to the waiting room after more than three hours of surgery, and informed us it was a very large hole that needed to be patched with a Gore-Tex patch. His lungs did not have the room to fully develop. Crushing. Short of death, we were now experiencing the "worst case." I was depressed beyond belief. Angry, confused, overwhelmed with guilt, you name it. How can he have a normal life? I remember thinking, is this all worth it? That was not like me, so this made me feel even more horrible that I would even have these thoughts. Scott, on the other hand, was an absolute rock. He stayed so positive the whole time. He of course, had his own emotions, but overall he was absolutely amazing. He was so supportive, comforting, loving, and so confident in Silas's strength.

He now had a big chest tube coming out of his rib cage to add to the collection of machines running his body, which was extremely painful, so they increased his pain medication. He still was not breathing on his own yet, either. How are we going to get all of these drugs out of his system after all of this? Is he likely to be a drug addict because of this? Despite all of the frustrations and concerns I had with Silas receiving so much medical intervention, overall the nurses, the doctors, the whole team were absolutely incredible. I truly believe there are some angels in disguise on that NICU floor.

We lived off campus at a vacation rental, as the Ronald McDonald house was full with a waiting list. Erik had set up all of our living situations for us, among so many other things. We were and are so blessed and deeply grateful for so much Love and support from both sides of our family, and friends too. Scott's side of the family made multiple road trips. Grandma Linda, Grandpa Tom, Uncle Mike, and Aunt Becky, came to hold baby Silas and supported us the whole way through. It was so incredibly helpful and comforting during such a challenging time. Lienne went to the hospital every day except maybe one or two days, she was truly amazing. She was such a comfort, incredibly dedicated big sister, and so full of Love. She would often sing to me when I was having a crying episode.

I will always remember the day 'I asked for more help.' I was in a "pumping room", pumping my milk for Silas to receive when he was ready, as I did every day. It was one of my deep crying sessions. I remember thinking we had the best of the best in Western Modern Medicine for him, feeling so incredibly grateful, and there were so many people praying for him, but he still needed a lot of help. I 'put the call out to the Universe' asking for more help. I remember being filled with "feeling"; I must have gone to my heart space. I already believed strongly in "Energetic Healing Arts," although I hadn't been thinking much about it up to that point, and did not have much direct experience. Do we get him to a point where we can take him somewhere, or do we find someone to come here to help him? Please help, I prayed, we need another miracle.

Within a few hours I received a phone call from Erik. It turns out that he and Kelly were having some friends over for dinner, Ola and Jason. Jason and Erik had started working in the fire department together many years prior. Erik and Kelly shared our story over dinner about how critical Silas was. Ola was emotionally touched by our story, and expressed, "Maybe my dad can help! Do you want me to call him?" She shared that her dad, Marek, was an "Energy Healer." Erik and Kelly (having believed and worked in Western Medicine) were very skeptical, and did not want to give me 'false hope.' Having known Jason for many years, Erik asked his opinion of Marek, and energy healing. Jason had been just as skeptical years before, until he started witnessing friends being healed after Marek performed energy healings; including some cases where modern medicine had given up on them. Indeed, Jason was now a believer in Marek's work. Erik thought, maybe there is something to this Energy Healing.

So, before giving 'false hope' to me without more information, Erik and Kelly gave the green light for Ola to call her dad right away. She explained the situation to Marek who had several questions about Silas and our family. Ola told Erik and Kelly that her dad said he needed to check with Silas's "angels and guides" to see if Silas was meant to be here. Marek explained, with Silas's soul permission, and if it were Silas's path to be here, then he could help. If it were his path to be here just a short time, then he would not be able to help and Silas may still die. Erik jokingly said it sounded pretty "Woo-Woo" and left a big "escape clause" if it did not work. Erik asked Ola if Marek would let them know which option it was. She said, "Yes, and my dad will call back."

About forty minutes later, Marek called back to speak with his daughter Ola, whom was still with Erik and Kelly. Erik said when Ola hung up the phone she was beaming. He of course asked what Marek had said. Ola responded, "He was able to check and communicate with Silas's angels and guides, and YES Silas is supposed to be here. He said he was able to do some (remote) energy work with the help of some other healers he knows, and that Silas is full of Gold Light now and will be fine from here on out." Kelly and Erik were stunned and did not know what to believe, or if they should risk getting my hopes up. They decided they did need to call me. I then received the phone call from my brother explaining what had just happened and repeated to me that Silas was full of Gold Light now, and would be fine from that point on.

I then shared with my brother that I had just been praying for a healer a few hours before. AMAZING! So full of hope and absolute gratitude, we felt incredible relief and joy. My mom and I remember 'dancing' around the little kitchen in our apartment. Was this really it?

Within just a few hours the milestones began and they did not stop. It started with his blood oxygen saturation, which had been critically low since birth and continued to be extremely low even after surgery. The hospital had explained that we were on a long road to recovery. Within several hours after the 'remote healing,' Silas's oxygen levels began to rise. Within every milestone, I had more and more confidence that Marek's help was truly making a huge difference in Silas's life. I remember the first day I could hold him, pure decadence. One morning our favorite nurse texted me to say his eyes were open! With these significant improvements, it became obvious it was outside of the "normal" healing speed for babies with CDH. The hospital staff kept warning us, "This is just a honeymoon phase, you are on a very long road to recovery, and there will be many set backs." We chose not to take these warnings and fears to heart. I was feeling strong again, and I chose to see the miracles that were happening.

The moment he started receiving my colostrum and breast milk through his feeding tube was absolutely perfect. The day his chest tube came out was another huge milestone, not only would he be in much less pain and not have to take so much pain medication, it also meant his lungs were functioning properly enough now. Not to mention how much easier it was to hold him. The day he was taken off of the breathing machine, he was a rock star breathing on his own! The milestones just kept coming, and everybody, including the hospital staff, was getting excited.

One of my personal favorites was the day he started nursing straight from the tap. This made his Papa proud too! Although he had to be on a specific schedule, hospital protocol, it was still wonderful. I asked every one of our nurses to talk to the "team" about letting me just sit in the rocking chair all day and nurse on demand. I was certain he would get enough milk if he could nurse whenever he desired. It was all a bit complicated with nursing at the beginning. One of the problems with babies who have this issue, is they spend a lot of extra energy latching on and suckling. So another hospital protocol was to supplement his feedings with formula. Now remember, we were the parents who asked for an "all natural" birth, this surly did not mean formula. Yet, another personal belief hurdle I needed to overcome. There were so many unnatural substances being poured into our beautiful new baby. I needed to just keep reminding myself he was alive, and we could clean him out, and do whatever we wanted as soon as he was all ours. We spent as much time as possible everyday, holding him and talking to him, simply just being with him. Lienne also wanted to see him, touch him, and hold him everyday, she was such a shining light for so many in that Intensive Care Nursery.

"Rooming In" day had arrived, the most exciting milestone yet! He had one last task to accomplish before going home. They finally agreed to let me just nurse him on demand. I would now be allowed to stay in a room with him, just the two of us with our own little bed, for three nights straight. Absolute bliss, I just cuddled, held, and nursed him for three whole days and nights straight. Scott and Lienne were able to visit a bit during the day while we were in our special room. If he gained weight every one of those three days on my breast milk alone, he would be able to go home. Apparently, babies with CDH have a really hard time gaining weight, because it takes so much energy for them to feed and digest their food. But he was doing beautifully already with his feedings and digestion, pooping and peeing no problem. Overall I felt confident. However, I was still a bit nervous about the whole process. One of his old nurses saw me walking into the room with Silas, and she said in absolute amazement, "Is that Silas? I can't believe it!"

I had also just recently spoken with our pediatrician back in Arcata area, and informed him Silas was probably coming home very soon. He responded, "That is absolutely incredible Laura. Usually these babies spend four to six months in the hospital and come home with a feeding tube and oxygen. One month and no feeding tube or oxygen, is really amazing." Needless to say, the whole team was impressed. We even heard the word "Miracle Baby" making its way around the hospital.

He did it! The day had arrived for us to take our Miracle Baby home. We took him home to our temporary San Francisco apartment on June 21, 2010. This was our wedding anniversary and summer solstice; what an absolutely perfect day to take our new baby home. We stayed one more night in our little apartment, and all journeyed back home to Humboldt County the next day. Grandma Flo, my mother, squeezed in the back seat between two full car seats and held Silas's hand on the way home. She was coming home with us to help with our new baby, what we had all been waiting for.

We had been home with Silas for about four months, when we were able to meet Marek in person for the first time. What immense gratitude and joy to see Marek hold and connect with Silas in person, for the first time. Here was my answered prayer in real life form. He is originally from Poland. In addition to distant (remote) healing and healing work at his home in Seattle area, Marek often travels to different areas where he is needed. While remaining open to donations or gifts from the heart, Marek does all of his healing work with nothing expected in return. We had invited him down for one of his healing weekends and sure enough he was needed and many wanted to meet with him in our area. He is pure LOVE, such a beautiful, compassionate, non-judging, human being. He is truly living and sharing his gift.

Silas is almost three years old now, and continues to be perfectly well and beautiful all the way around. He continues to enjoy nursing as if it were his first time. Every single check up he has had since being released from the hospital Silas has been reported as, "A perfectly healthy, normal, growing boy." What an incredible healing and spiritual journey so many of us have been on and continue to be on, since Silas's birth and meeting Marek. I have profound Gratitude for the beautiful miracles we have experienced. My life and perspective on life, has positively changed and expanded in so many ways, and continue to do so. Words cannot express the deep joy, appreciation, and Love I feel for both of my children every single day. Seeing, believing and appreciating the Miracles of Life, Modern Medicine, Ancient Wisdom, and Loving prayers is now the way I joyfully choose to live.

SEVENTH PLACE WINNER

CREATIVITY CHANGED MY LIFE

ANNIE RIESS
UNITY, SASKATCHEWAN. CANADA

"I guess your son got his creativity from you." My friend stated. I wanted to shake my head vehemently—but I stood there as her words soaked deep into my soul. Yes, my son was creative—but me? Creative? Was I ever going to accept it? Would I stop trying to overlook it and just receive it for what it was, a 'gift'? Why did I continue to try and run from it?

Being creative filled my days the first few years of life. I loved to make things and coloring was one of my favorite pastimes. One day when I was about three, my bachelor uncle came to visit and I was thrilled to color him a beautiful picture. I proudly carried it over and placed it in his hands expectantly. He glanced at it and said: "You need to learn how to color."

I was shocked. Learn how to color? I already knew how, didn't I?

My uncle continued his instruction. "You need to color going all the same way. See? You are going this way and that way."

I felt a big rock in my tummy . . . I felt so sad . . . I looked down at my little red shoes . . . what did he mean?

My dad must've seen the look on my face and came to my recue. "She's just a little girl. She'll learn. Don't be so hard on her."

Then my tummy really hurt, and my little heart ached for my poor uncle. Maybe if I didn't color anymore then, no one would get hurt.

One night my mom was playing the piano so we could have a family sing-a-long. I was young, but I remember desperately begging God to let me be able to sit down and play a tune. I went to the piano several times in the following weeks just to try to pick out a tune. Bit by bit I realized I was able to play little tunes. It was quite a few years before I could play for the family, but I had a lot of fun trying to learn.

I was the second oldest in a family of six. We grew up on a farm and life was busy with lots of 'chores' for us to do. Whenever we had some free time—it was entertaining to amuse ourselves with what we could come up with—and acting out a short play I had written was often our entertainment for the day.

How I loved to write up plays and poems for my younger siblings to 'act out'. We would put on a 'concert' for mom and dad and anyone else who would listen.

Enterprising is an area of creativity as well. I was always dreaming up things we could do to make money. We started a 'manufacturing club', with our cousins. We braided old baler twine, from the bales to make great ropes to 'sale'. Yes, using my imagination to be creative changed my life and gave all of us a little more joy in life.

My sister was a year and a half older than I, so she had started taking piano lessons a year before I did. I caught up to her in just a few short months. My parents and teacher were astounded and so pleased—until my teacher found out that I could not read music. I was simply playing, by ear, what I had heard my sister play. My teacher was infuriated. I can still recall the awful feeling of humiliation, sitting on the piano bench with my head bowed down as big scalding tears dripped off my chin and onto my hands.

I'm sure my teacher never meant to be hurtful—but her words stabbed deep into my heart, as she told me: "Your conduct is not unacceptable! You will never be able to play piano 'properly' if you can't read. How could you do this? All this time, I thought you were doing so well."

I felt like a complete failure. I had only wanted to play the pieces like my big sister—it didn't matter to me 'how' I played, but I did not want to be a 'failure' in the eyes of my teacher either.

"I'm so . . . sor . . . ry . . . I'll wo . . . rk . . . harder . . ." was all I could say. I really had no idea what I had done wrong. All I knew was my teacher was angry with me.

I could also play these same pieces with 'extra' notes and different timing. I was sure glad my teacher didn't know that! My creativity had really hurt me, (at least for the time being) because I was a child who wanted to please those around me. I lost all desire to play; practicing became real drudgery as I struggled to learn how to read.

One day, that summer mom came to me and said: "We have decided to change teachers. It will be much more convenient to go to a teacher who lives closer to Grandma. Dad has known this Mrs. Robertson for years and says she is a very nice lady. I'm sure you will enjoy lessons with her."

So, a bend in the road brought new thoughts and ideas to my world. My new teacher loved my musical playing and even encouraged me to play by 'ear'. In fact, she played my pieces for me, so I could 'copy' her. There was still a 'small' drawback—since Mrs. Robertson encouraged me to play by ear, I did not learn to read notes well. Even though I have taken lessons as an adult, I still struggle somewhat. Reading is not my 'first' language—I lack confidence—I have not acknowledged my creativity as a gift. Is this part of the reason I hesitate to claim my creativity?

I continued to play a lot by ear and over time I could pick out little tunes. One day the regular pianist for our little country church was ill. "What hymns and choruses can you play?" I was asked. I knew several, so that is what the congregation sang that day. I was only eleven years old. This was the beginning of many years of playing for church. (We attend a larger church and I still play. Sometimes I wonder if God blessed me with the ability to play by ear long before I was born, or did he hear the heart cry of a little girl who wanted to just sit down and play? Either way, I have learned, it takes a lot of work to develop that raw talent.)

After high school, I worked for a short time in a bakery. One day the manager came to me and said, "I have noticed you are artistic and have a 'flair' for decorating the cupcakes and gingerbread men. Sometime, I would like to teach you to decorate the wedding cakes."

I was surprised, but pleased, though I never thought of decorating things as being artistic. Icing the things in the bakery simply added variety to my days. Creativity was opening new doors once again.

I married my husband and moved to the family farm to live with him. Money was tight, so I had absolutely no budget to decorate with. Everything I did had to be either from things given to me, or 'bought' at a thrift store, but I was determined to make our house into a home. I fixed up each room. I scrubbed then, painted with whatever color of paint I could get my hands on. I sewed 'new' drapery out of old ones and matched colors to suit the rooms. I did everything I could to give it a 'homey' touch, without spending any money. I was delighted when my husband's sister was visiting and said. "You have a real knack for decorating. The house looks wonderful. It looks much bigger and brighter." Creativity had saved the day.

Looking back my favorite part is—what to me at the time—was the worst part. We did not have indoor plumbing and so we had an outhouse. I had grown up with running water, and had assumed everyone in the western world had such a necessity. Well, since we didn't, I was determined to be innovative and have the best looking outhouse anyone had ever seen. The outside of it was faded a bit, but it would do. The inside was downright ugly. It was old parched wood. With a brush and roller, I painted it bright yellow, then I took a piece of wallpaper and cut out the large orange and red flowers with long green stems. I pasted them here and there over the walls to make my own private little indoor garden. I cut little tiny green 'curtains' and sewed them to fit the air vents. Last, but not least, I 'splurged' and bought a small three by five foot, new indoor/outdoor carpet. It truly was a work of art—it raised my spirits each time I had to 'visit' out there.

A few years later when our son was born, people were generous and between gifts and the thrift store we made out all right. When our daughter was born and we were still poor, while we continued to wait for that 'crop' that would make us rich, I knew I had to use my imagination to make those clothes for boys into little outfits suitable for a girl. I bought some pretty lace and butterflies and flowers to 'remake' them into something feminine. The jogging suits were the easiest. A 'crest' of a pink kitten turned a pale blue suit into a girl's outfit. Lace around the collar and cuffs changed a dress shirt into a blouse. Surprisingly they all turned out quite beautiful. I was inspired to continue to be innovative.

As my family grew, I began to look for ways to develop their abilities. Of course music was of interest to them as well, since we always had music in our home. I heard about a lady in town who taught the 'Suzuki Method'. This method was started in Japan with Dr. Suzuki. It is known as the "mother-tongue" method. It differs from traditional methods because it is built on learning music the same way a child learns to speak. When a child begins to speak, he or she has heard their mother tongue for approximately one to two years, and then gradually they begin to speak what she or he has heard. Later, the child will be taught to read. I was astounded! Finally, someone understood me. That is exactly what I had wanted to do all those years ago when my teacher was so upset with me for copying what I had heard my sister play.

I went to see if this teacher had room in her schedule to teach my children. I was devastated to learn that she was moving away! Oh, no, just when I thought I'd found someone who could understand my way of making music.

"You can go to the city and take the training, to teach this method yourself." Melanie told me.

"But how? I have a family and my life is so busy."

"You will need to practice and send in a tape of your playing, then if you are accepted, you will have a short training period, in the city. The rest is just practice time, which you can do on your own." She replied.

And so it was that I 'learned' to teach how to play the piano—first by ear and then by note. Due to the creativity God has blessed me with, it has been my joy to teach 'Suzuki' piano for the past twenty-five plus years!

Writing was another avenue of creativity I had enjoyed as a youngster, but due to time restraints while farming and raising a family I had dropped it altogether. One day I decided to send in a write-up about Christmas. The paper accepted it. I sent a few more small write-ups to a farm paper and they published them—almost all of them. I longed to take writing courses so I could understand how to write better so they would accept all of them. (I have since learned that rejection is a big part of the writing world—ha!)

Times continued to be tough on the farm so the government decided to pay for 'retraining' so farmers would be able to diversify their income. I received a copy of the various programs and looked over the long list of things to train for. There were things like; Business Certificate, Hairstylist, Plumbing and Pipefitting, Pharmacy Technician, Computers . . . nothing there was of interest to me. What would interest me? What could I do? As I continued to research and talk with our local college, I found out I could take writing courses. Writing? That is exactly what I had been dreaming of. With money being so tight I never dreamt I'd ever be able to take a course. Over the next few of years, I was blessed to be able to complete fifteen courses through the local college.

One day while working on a writing class, I came to a list of things creative people like to do. I was astonished to see that it included numerous things I took pleasure in doing. The list included things like baking, cooking, singing, painting, decorating, sewing, and playing a musical instrument. Maybe I am creative? I thought as I went back over the list.

Baking was the one that really caught my attention. Baking? For years I had loved to bake. It gave me joy just to 'put together' something for my family. How I loved to pull out the bowls and gather the ingredients. I took great pride in being able to turn out a beautiful product. Although I am not a perfectionist, I had learned to be one when it came to baking, so that it would turn out well. For a few years, when our children were young, we had joined the local farmer's market and baking was something we did a lot of. I had never thought of that as being creative—yet it certainly was. I would crack a couple of eggs, pour some oil into the measuring cup, bend down to see exactly when it reached 'the line', then carefully beat it in with the eggs. Sugar, was an important ingredient and like flour, it was best measured by taking a knife and carefully leveling the top of the measuring cup. Incorporate some leveling agent, such as yeast, or baking powder or soda—and with only a few changes in ingredients—I would come up with a pan of warm buns, crunchy chocolate chip cookies, or a birthday cake. Was that not being creative? Cooking was another thing on the list I had not contemplated as being creative. Cooking was just something that needed to be done. We needed to eat, and so it fell to me to be the one to cook. Sure, I 'didn't mind' it—but was I expressing myself through it? I guess it does take a certain amount of creativity to be able to always be trying new dishes and 'enjoy' cooking.

Crafts were on this list. I had thoroughly enjoyed making birthday and all occasion cards for my family and friends for years. I saved old pictures and took classes to learn how to write gothic lettering and calligraphy on the cards. This was another area I had to admit took a certain amount of creativity. Sure, I had always thought I had done it because it was much more meaningful and provided a nice card for a nominal price. Now, I had to admit, I also did it to satisfy my 'need' to be creative. Was that the real reason I made cards?

Another writing class suggested reading Julia Cameron's book, *The Artist's Way*. In it she recommends every creative person take at least an hour each week to do something creative. I began to find lots of ways to express my creativity. When going for a walk, for years, I had saved nice flat stones, thinking someday I'll do something with them. Well, 'someday' had arrived and I choose three of my favorite rocks and painted flowers on them—I felt 'fulfilled' to be doing something relaxing—something I truly loved. It had been years since I had 'nourished' my creativity, and it felt so invigorating!

I continued to send freelance stories to magazines and papers and surprisingly they continued to accept many of them. In 2008 I saw an advertisement to win a week in New York at the famous Guideposts Writers Workshop. I entered the contest and won a spot! Going up against over 5,000 entries, and I was one of only fifteen writers selected for the workshop. No one was more surprised than I. Was this also a part of being creative?

When they had called to tell me I had won—I was stupefied and the fellow on the other end of the line said: "You don't sound too excited. Are you sure you want to accept this?" I really wasn't sure I did. Going to New York was going to be a big change for a farm girl from Saskatchewan. Thirty years earlier, at the age of nineteen, I had had the opportunity to go to New York to model some kind of face creams and makeup but I had turned it down. I was not interested. Now, at my age with beauty quickly fading, my only hope of going to New York would have to be something else, and here was creativity giving me the chance of a lifetime—would I accept?

My husband, Ken was far more excited about the trip than I was. As writers, we were going to be staying dorm-style at picturesque Wainwright House. This meant I would have to travel alone, since only Workshop participants could stay there and, I was the only Canadian to have won a spot. With Ken's support, I graciously accepted the prize and began to make arrangements to go. We had not been apart for more than a day in our thirty plus years of marriage, and Ken began to 'worry' how he'd survive without me. I had some very real misgivings as well.

The big day arrived in early October and he drove me to the airport. When I turned to kiss him goodbye at the security gates, there were big tears rolling down his cheeks.

"Oh, Ken, it's not that bad." I said brushing his cheek with my hand. "I'll only be gone the week."

"Are you sure you can manage?" He questioned me once again. "You've got to pay attention to where you're going. You'll end up lost in some airport, and I'll never see you again." Ken always was one to over-exaggerate things, but I still felt badly leaving him standing there feeling so helpless.

Later I wrote in my journal. "Off to a rocky start. When I stood in line at security and could still see Ken with the tears rolling down his cheeks, I also had to fight for control. At security, they held me up by examining and re-examining my carry-on. Then they conferred with each other and examined it again. Finally they let me go. I rushed away before they would change their mind. I hurried so fast; I forgot to get my jacket and liquids out of the second basket. (Don't tell Ken)

I went up the escalator to Air Canada waiting area, and over to the window to wave back at Ken. He mouthed, "Where's your jacket?" and made the motion of putting a coat over his shoulders. I nodded as though I knew where it was and scurried back to find it. Fortunately, it was still there. So I gathered up my things and went to the Air Canada area. I was feeling proud of myself for finding the Air Canada gate—but a few minutes later I noticed there weren't many people at our gate and a lot more down a little further. I checked my ticket. I was at the wrong gate! (That is two mistakes and I'm not even out of the city yet) Better be much more careful!

I was extremely careful after that and things went smoothly. I enjoyed every minute of my time in New York. There was so much to learn at the workshop, and I made many new friends. In true dorm style, we giggled like schoolgirls over everything, and stayed up half the night talking. Creativity had blessed me again.

As you can see, creativity has really changed my life—so why have I been afraid to truly embrace it? I have asked myself this many times and it is precisely why I have chosen to write this memoir. I wanted to probe my thoughts and feelings to see why I feel as I do. What I have seen is that my creativity has indeed made me different. In the past being creative sometimes wounded me and so I lacked confidence to use my creativity. Yet, I have also been blessed abundantly by it. Consequently, I can be inclined to feel 'second-rate' because I do things in an unusual way—or I can joyfully incorporate my creativity to do things distinctly differently!

I join with the Psalmist in saying; "You created my inmost being; you knit me together in my mother's womb. I praise you because I am fearfully and wonderfully made; your works are wonderful, I know that full well." (Psalm 139: 13 & 14) That is what I choose to believe—I am 'fearfully and wonderfully made'.

So, I have embraced my creativity. My friend was correct; my son is creative . . . and so am I. I have come to accept my creativity as a blessing. God, the greatest Creator of all time created me (and you) in a unique and special way. To get the most out of life, we need to embrace the one-of-a-kind people we were meant to be.

CREATIVITY—TICKET TO A BETTER PLACE

JULIA GREGOR
CONCORD, CA

P ink is my favorite color. I try to see life through rose-colored glasses. When I got the phone call, I saw red.

"Cathy, you have to come and bail me out," my brother stated.

"What did you do?"

"Nothing."

This is the story of how my Vietnam-veteran brother flushed his medications down the toilet, smashed his neighbor's windshield, beat up his roommate, and—as if that weren't enough—wrote a letter to the County Assessor threatening to kill him if he didn't confess that he had stolen from the government for years (he hadn't), and turned my life upside down. And how creativity righted it again.

Twenty-five years ago I became my brother's keeper, by default; Bill had sucked the life out of my mother with whom he had lived, while my other two siblings self-servingly denied that mental illness exists, telling themselves that our brother was "just a bum". Since then, I had single-handedly fielded his five to ten daily phone calls, righted his dysfunctional roommate relationships after he booted them out, gave shelter to his un-housebroken dog while he vacationed at the Veteran's Administration Hospital, and interfaced with his various doctors and social workers.

What about family, you ask. Family? That nuclear group that's supposed to be there when you need them? I've spent my adult life repressing the lack thereof. My mom raised her four free-spirited children on her own while my father, a disabled World War II veteran, took breaks away from us to contemplate his navel in the psychiatric ward of the Palo Alto V.A. Hospital. Dad left the seminary to join the Navy in World War II, meet my mom, and have a nervous breakdown. When she wasn't saying, "Your father is a good example of a bad example," she'd mumble that he missed his calling as a Jesuit priest.

If necessity is the mother of invention, then creativity is its stepmother. My mom was the mistress of making something out of nothing. We were very resourceful when it came to entertaining ourselves. My brother's forte was concocting excuses for keeping the dogs, cats, and lizards my mother forbade us to have but somehow stayed. I read; I sewed; I imagined. We never really wanted for anything. We saw the bright side of life, which, under the circumstances, may have been a manifestation of the crazy gene that's in our DNA.

While my family has its share of certifiable nuts, we also have our cock-eyed optimists, like my pragmatic Aunt Mary, who, when her husband announced he was leaving her to marry her best friend, said, "Whatever makes them happy." The eldest of my mother's sisters, she lived twenty years longer than the others, probably because she seemed to take everything in stride. I had fine examples of what to be and what not to be.

When I found myself approaching my "Golden Years," I looked around at those who were ensconced in Retirement . . . my predecessors and models. I don't know if their hormones deserted them or they just had too much time to think about their troubles, but—shudder—I wanted to be in a different place mentally, emotionally and physically. I loved them, but I didn't want to be them. Fortunately, I had the skills implanted in me by a lifetime of necessity and my mother who, in response to her sisters' remarks about her children's behavior, said we were "free thinkers." She did not want to stifle our imagination. Creativity would be my ticket to a different place.

Transitioning from a career I had spent the major part of my adult life developing was scary. As a real estate broker, I had written a newsletter for years and (speaking of making something out of nothing) included stories about the silly things my dogs did. Soon, that space-filler became the most popular column in the monthly. Neighbors would stop me on the street and ask, "What has Bubbles done lately?" My husband was recognized only when he was walking "the poodle from hell" and "the deaf Dalmatian," their monikers in the tales. Someone suggested I publish their antics, and the book bug bit me. Talk about a leap of faith . . .

Should I take the time away from producing income to indulge my creative spirit and write a book about two aberrant dogs? Should I turn down listings and write instead, thereby diminishing the family's income, which, since I don't cook or clean, largely established my worth as a human being? While pondering these questions, I took some action and submitted my query and sample chapters to several agents and publishers. In response, I received six rejection letters. Unlike in real estate, I knew it would take more than twenty "no's" to get to "yes." And I never liked the rejection part of real estate. Should I self-publish? I needed some divine intervention here.

From the day I was born, when my mother placed a bouquet of violets in the hand of the Saint Mary statue at Saint Joseph's Catholic Hospital in Chicago and prayed to her that I would never know want, I've had a special bond with Mary. So I prayed . . .

I began to get messages:

- A horoscope that read: Your talents for wordsmithing and research come into increasing play as the year progresses.
- A fortune cookie with the message: Your genuine talent will find its way to success.
- A greeting card that caught my husband's eye in a shop as I was anguishing aloud over spending the time on this project—an angel with her head cocked, pleading: Tell your story

Clearly, Saint Mary was speaking to me.

And then I got the phone call. Which was preceded by an eerie silence of twenty-four hours, during which I would normally have had at least five phone calls from Bill. "You have to get me out of here. They aren't giving me my meds. They took my dog."

Over the years, Bill had been diagnosed as schizophrenic, manic-depressive, bipolar, paranoid—you name it, some psychiatrist said he had it. One even thought he had Asperger's Syndrome, which was Bill's favorite diagnosis because he thought imitating Forest Gump was really cute. Post-Traumatic Stress Disorder was the one he hung his hat and "Vietnam Veteran" jacket on every day as he cultivated his persona: Disabled Vet. Several therapists told me that his behavior was not just a manifestation of the illness it was an art form he had skillfully developed. It worked for him and he knew how to work it. He mastered passive aggression, and as the professionals counseled me, knew just which buttons to push.

I realized there wasn't any point in calling my other two brothers to powwow; Bill who? So I spent the next twenty-four hours determining that he would be charged with three felonies at his arraignment, coordinating his V.A.-prescribed medications with the jail nurse, and bailing his dog out of doggie jail. If he went to prison, the V.A. would cut off his benefits and the little condo we had bought for him would go away, as would the equity we'd built, unless we sold it. And then there'd be no place for Bill to return to. No way would any landlord accept him. And I was in the middle of writing and publishing my book, Tales of a Codependent Pet Owner! A light-hearted, humorous book! I had already paid CreateSpace $849 and I had only six months left on our contract.

Writing became my cross and my salvation. I knew that if I didn't finish I would never forgive myself—or my brother. Which is stupid—I have control over my life; no one else does unless I allow him or her to control me. Was I going to let the quagmire that was my brother's life swallow me up? Hell, no! So I prayed some more.

I got up each morning and asked for divine guidance and inspiration. I unplugged the phone, ignored my voice mail, did not look at e-mail, and wrote for three hours. I was blessed that I could get away with that, and often found that the "problem" fixed itself by the time I got involved. My mind, which is prone to wandering and ruminating on the current idea du jour, focused.

Amazing . . . the concentration required to block my family out produced typewritten pages. I saw progress. I laughed. I was in a better mood and more able to handle the rest of my life in the afternoon. Even the technology challenge (dealing with WordSmasher and uploading the manuscript to CreateSpace's publishing platform) was overcome. The whole mind control exercise was a vacation from life.

Meanwhile, back at the jail ranch, the legal process began. While I believed that Bill brought a lot of trouble on himself, I had accepted that he wasn't normal to begin with. (As a kid, he once refilled my water bottle with Clorox and laughed as I took a swig—one of many telltale signs.) Vietnam just nailed his coffin shut. I knew that if someone didn't show his or her face at the court hearings (in which he appeared shackled and handcuffed in a holding cage), if someone didn't communicate daily with the jail staff, explain him to the nurse, and put money onto his canteen tab so he could buy cigarettes and bribes for his new best friends, my brother would fall into the abyss of our underfunded legal system. Time away from writing my book . . .

So, in a lapse of reason, I called the "family." "Hi, there. Hey, I could really use some help. Can you come down and appear at this hearing so I can brush my teeth and comb my hair?"

Brother #2: "You know Bill's a bum. He's always been a bum. He's getting what he deserves."

Brother #3: "Well, Cath, he's made his bed; let him lie in it."

Despite Bill's numerous diagnoses of mental illness, to my family he was still "just a bum". So I soldiered on. Alone. My husband was a tremendous support, but he's an engineer. Left-brained. After retiring from the Navy (his brain still intact) he went into environmental work, cleaning up polluters. I remember standing at the door one morning, waving goodbye to him, thinking, "You're so lucky. All you have to do every day is design a remediation plan for a defunct nuclear power plant. I have to write." And deal with my brother.

My mother used to say, "You can't think about two things at once." Wrong! As I wrote, I fantasized about murdering my brothers. Which is not Christian. Which I knew Saint Mary would not approve of and would therefore not intercede in my supplication to get published. Plus, I want to go to heaven someday, and I'd been taught that to get there, you have to love and forgive everyone. This caused me great anxiety.

Loving Bill wasn't the issue. Jesus said the hardest ones to love are the ones who need it the most, and I could go along with that most of the time. But the other two—that was a stretch. Maybe I could get out on a technicality: they both had wives who loved them (or said they did), so why did they need my love? Jesus also said, "As I have loved you, so you must love one another." Big loophole—I know He didn't like the moneychangers. He also said that to forgive is divine and, God knows, I'm not divine.

I guess my subconscious didn't buy these excuses, and I ended up with a great big bout of guilt-induced writer's block. Payback from God.

Saint Mary to the rescue! I happened to be spinning the dial on the car radio one day and inadvertently landed on The Catholic Channel. I never listen to that station; it makes me feel guilty. But before I could grab the knob again, I heard these words: "Forgiveness is not reconciliation. It's giving up Revenge, Resentment, and Retribution." Hmmmm . . . I never really wanted revenge or retribution; I'd have to work on resentment. If I could master these three Rs, I wouldn't have to worry about the fourth: Reconciliation! My interest was piqued.

The program featured Dr. Ross Porter, a noted counselor in Christian spirituality, who was discussing the virtue of forgiveness. He said, "You don't have to continue in a hurtful relationship or condone or forget." I could do that! I could block those two out of my life! Then, as if speaking directly to me, he said, "Humor is a virtue." From his lips to my ears . . . I could be forgiven.

My writer's block evaporated, and so Tales of a Codependent Pet Owner came to be. It went live on Amazon on Thanksgiving Day, 2011. How appropriate! My horoscope for that week read, "A much anticipated development comes to pass. Savor the moment of triumph because this justifies all of your hard work." The Divine had granted my prayers.

Meanwhile, the struggles with Bill continued. I got his bail reduced from $50,000 to zero. He was released on his own recognizance pending trial, but his driver's license had been revoked. All the court appearances, the doctors appointments, shopping, everything, was my job. It could always be worse, I told myself (a mantra I adopted early in life).

To add to my misery, real estate had become a major pain in the rear. The local market had caught up with the foreclosure and short sale circus, and it just wasn't fun anymore: three times the amount of work, ten times the annoyance, and much of it was pro bono. I didn't want to sap one more brain cell than I had to dwelling on real estate or my brother. I needed to get my mind into a happy rut. One that would, again, block out the negativity around me and give me joy. I would write! But about what?

I had run out of dog stories. I needed a topic that would engage people as much as pets do. What else has the same drama/angst/potential to make readers laugh? It was staring me right in the face: technology! And thus was hatched my blog, A Little Bit Off—Right Brain in a Left Brain World. My husband became MyHusbandTheEngineer. When I wasn't voicing my frustration with the latest computer software or hardware I was forced to adapt to, I wrote about absurdities in the news. The dogs made cameo appearances, but they weren't doing as many naughty things lately—maybe I'd trained them?! More likely they were just getting old.

The tricky thing about blogging is that if you don't post regularly you look like a dabbler. You can't fudge the dates on your posts. If I wanted to show the public that I was worth following, I had to produce consistently, and I was having so much fun with it that I wanted my blog to morph into a new career. Writing a humor blog requires time—revision after revision. How was I going to do that and deal with both my brother and my real estate business? I prayed.

My first sign came by way of a horoscope: If one source of income ends, do not worry—a new one likely will be quick to follow. When a job offers you a paycheck but nothing more, it will be easy to see how it holds you back from developing your full potential. (I came to see that time is relative, metaphysically speaking.)

My next sign was less spiritual. Four families whose parents had sworn they would list their homes with me when mom and dad went to the Retirement Villa in the Sky, and who spent hours pumping me for information because I am the neighborhood specialist, subsequently listed the family home with their friends, not me. In the space of two months, I'd had it! But could I really write funny stuff?

And then my eyes fell on this passage in the Bible (Exodus, 4:11—God to Moses, who didn't think he had the ability to lead the people out of Egypt and was trying to talk his way out of it): "I will help you speak and will teach you what to say." Surely God was telling me that He'd put words in my mind and I could write humor!

And so, I write. Life still goes on in that parallel universe. My brother was forgiven his sins by a most empathetic lady judge and District Attorney. His public defender was a beautiful woman from the south, whose own son had served in Iraq and who, when I thanked her profusely for making my brother her personal cause, told me that we were brought together for a reason and that, "God works in mysterious ways."

My loyal real estate clients tolerate my writing hibernations and wait for me. They also laugh at my writing!

Serendipity? I don't believe there's anything accidental in the events of my life; I've seen God's hand in every one of them. I've been blessed with the opportunity to engage with brilliant, inspiring, helpful professionals and novices in the writing community. I will never be Dave Barry (I prefer wine), but my columns have appeared in a number of newspapers and national magazines (divine intervention?). Creativity has been my passport out of anguish into a world that I can sustain as long as I live. If I lose my mind, I'll just get funnier! Retire? Are you kidding? Where else would I get fodder for my stories?

Just yesterday, as I drove away from a writers' club meeting, I slowed and stopped at an intersection. There, before my eyes, was a bumper sticker that read, "You are good. Jesus Christ." I hope He means my writing.

A TIE FOR EIGHTH PLACE WINNER

THE GODDESS WAKES

ANGELA LA VOIE
CENTENNIAL, CO

As long as I can remember, I was subtly aware of the importance of creativity (helping to improve brain function and unlock our emotions, for example), but it wasn't until I sustained a traumatic brain injury as part of a near-fatal whitewater accident that I understood the power of creativity to transform and heal us.

Whitewater rafting in my home state of Colorado, I was ejected from my boat, landing in a whirlpool so powerful that it pinned me against some boulders and whatever else that lay beneath the unseen water's surface. The force of the water sent me ricocheting, my helmeted head repeatedly striking the boulders. When I freed myself from the whirlpool and got back to my raft, I didn't know I'd hit my head. It would be almost a year later that my husband would recall that part of the accident; I still don't remember it. Back in the boat on that unseasonably cold July morning, it was my right hip, my left shoulder and my right elbow that were smarting the most. Back on land, I felt beat up by the cold water and the rocks, but nothing seemed broken or very serious. My doctor diagnosed me with a concussion, along with an assortment of other injuries. She said the concussion could be sustained just from the force of my brain's movement in my skull. That was creepy enough. When my symptoms didn't heal after a few weeks, I sought further evaluation from trauma specialists and neurologists. My physiatrist, a doctor who specializes in pain and rehabilitative medicine, told me my progress would be measured in years, that the one-year mark would be a significant milestone. "But my primary care physician said it would be a few weeks?" I said. "Really? She said that?" He exhaled loudly. I couldn't tell if he was doubting me or the professional competency of the other physician. His prognosis confused me. It took me several re-hashes of the conversation to realize the physiatrist's prognosis was likely accurate, if lacking in bedside manner. It took a while for me to grasp my new reality.

My brain injury symptoms went on for months, even years, long after the MRI showed that my brain injury had healed. While all of this is fairly common, this information came about piecemeal. As a former health journalist, I was used to talking with medical professionals and making sense of medical information. I would eventually learn that my situation is unfortunately a common state of affairs with brain injuries. They are often poorly or under diagnosed, and treatment is cobbled together except in the most severe cases. But I wouldn't know about this until later.

What I knew early on is that I had vise-gripping headaches for months that were only dulled with medication and I was not one to pop pills lightly. I had constant repetitive nightmares for a year. I had vestibular symptoms that made it difficult to walk on a dirt trail or even a lawn, even though I could swing a subdued tree pose in yoga. Riding in a car, it looked like the houses, trees and horses on the roadside were jumping out at me. Dappled sunlight filtering through a tree's leaves or reflecting off a lake's surface felt like tiny daggers. The harsh lights and endless rows of products in grocery stores and big box retailers felt like they were poking me in the eyes and gave me a sense of vertigo. With all of this, it was hard to give any attention to my broken tailbone.

Initially, my job was to be as still as I could and rest for the most of the day except for my physical therapy. Jamie, my physical therapist, taught me to look at my brain usage like a bank account. Each day, I had to balance physical therapy and brain therapy with everyday tasks like fixing lunch. Eventually, I could do more and at least watch a little TV or read a breezy romance. As a lifelong reader and writer, I was lonely for the ability to arrange words in a cohesive way and to read without missing, forgetting or not understanding pertinent information. I learned the back pages of People magazine featured a puzzle with two photographs that were identical except for a number of details that were manipulated by its graphic designers. The puzzle consists of recognizing that the red belt in one image is replaced by a gray belt in the companion photograph, that the tattoo on a man's shoulder in one photo is on his forearm in another. This puzzle I would have considered an amusing pastime previously now served as an exercise in rehabilitation. Even my speech language pathologist agreed.

As a former health journalist, an athlete and somewhat compulsive knowledge seeker, I was eager to do anything I could to get better. I kept pestering my health team for what else I could do. Outside of their instructions for rest and physical and cognitive rehab, they said the rest was up to me. Keep doing what you're doing was the universal theme. Keep doing what you're doing was the mantra.

Well what was I doing exactly? Was there something specific I was doing? A long-time yogini and hobbyist yoga instructor, I knew it wasn't yoga that was helping me, although I do think it played a role in saving me from drowning. My yogic training may have helped me to stay calm and breathe as I struggled literally to keep my head above the icy water. In the water, I remember prompting myself to let my body act as a reed and bend with the current rather than get sucked under by the water's force. Back on shore, though, I had to give up teaching yoga after trying to teach through a broken tailbone and other injuries for a while. Even doing what poses I could and verbally cueing the rest, I found yoga made my head spin. I wanted yoga to be part of my healing, especially because I just quit my job as a project manager a few weeks before my accident to take a yoga sabbatical and possibly open a local yoga studio. But yoga was no friend to my brain injury and fell by the wayside. I instead focused on the movements my physical therapist taught me, a combination of traditional physical therapy, Pilates and Franklin method movement.

During this time, my head functioned something like a weather vane. In what I'll call my head's neutral state, my head felt like a waterlogged tennis ball. A headache signaled too much effort, not enough sleep, not enough food, too much neck pain or any number of things. My head buzzed with something like spidery sense when there was an error (wrong change counted back to me or missing someone's birthday) or when I needed to be cautious about someone else's behavior, like a lie or a slight. My head would buzz in warning, and I would have to figure out what was amiss. Maybe Spider-Man knew something about brain injuries. But my brain also reached a happy, healing vibration and a sense of connectedness when I was able to piece together lost memories, make a new association, or attain a sharper level of cognitive clarity. I searched to discover the activities that promoted this feeling. Gardening and decorating seemed to fit the bill. I scheduled a series of home improvements to help me get better and monitor their effects. I consulted Jamie, my physical therapist, for her opinion. The gardening would also help me with my spine and my core, she noted. I decided to give it a go. My husband and I had purchased a colonial fixer-upper less than a year before my accident, so the projects were lying in wait.

Seeking pillows and draperies for our family room, I watched design shows on television, glanced through home and garden magazines, and the Web sites of home goods and textile retailers. Soon, I began to recognize the objects in design-show "room reveals" on television. I could recognize the rug, the dishware, and the lamp that I'd seen elsewhere. My brain buzzed its happy, harmonious buzz in these moments of recognition. I recognized my own dinner plates in a television commercial. I recognized coffee tables from retailer's Web sites in glossy spreads in home and garden magazines. It became something of a game. I researched well beyond my own home's needs for the excitement of being able to recognize the pattern of a textile in a settee in a room featured on a magazine's cover.

When the tile installer failed to show up or call the day he was supposed to start tiling my family room, I'd decided to tile the room myself. I'd laid tile before and I'd had my fill of contractors for a while. So I went to the Home Depot and took a tile class. I asked the instructor questions after class. His wife had sustained a head injury in a car accident several years earlier. He understood why I needed to tile the floor. I reviewed my detailed notes and wrote a plan for the floor, something I wouldn't have needed to do before my accident. My instructor helped me choose a pattern in which to lay out the tiles that would look appealing as it eventually stretched through four rooms of my home. The first day of the family room project, I laid eleven tiles, my husband handling the tile saw for me. I didn't trust my hand-eye coordination enough yet, though I'd used a tile saw before. I just figured out where to place the tiles, specified the needed cuts and laid the tiles in place. Between the cognitive effort of the calculations I needed to do to lay out the floor and the strain on my back, neck and hips from laying the tile, I couldn't move for a few days afterwards. Signs of the athlete I'd previously been were missing, except perhaps for my stubborn determination to keep going. In between less demanding projects and other responsibilities, it took me several months to finish that floor. I felt sorry for the future homeowner who wishes to replace that flooring. Those tiles won't make for easy demolition. They are quite solidly in place, even if it took me forever.

I had made something beautiful and I was eager to capture that feeling of accomplishment again. Several months later, when Spring came, I set out to re-do a side yard, a derelict garden that seemed to have been re-planted several times by the previous homeowners and drew the nastiest tangle of shrubs, weeds, grasses and flowers and which made it impossible to sleep with the master bedroom windows open in warm weather because of the intense allergy attacks the derelict plantings caused. What started as a simple paver patio with some raised herb and vegetable beds for a potager, or kitchen garden, blossomed into a serenity garden with a sun patio, flowering ornamental trees, climbing roses and clematis, and xeriscaped plantings surrounding a tiny pond and waterfall. Sketching the designs, selecting furnishings and collaborating with the landscaper on the plantings taught me I could transform both my surroundings and my inner state of being. The waterfall was modeled after a beautiful spa I'd visited in the Colorado mountains. That weed-infested side yard became the place where I spent at least a couple hours each day. I completed the serenity garden by the first anniversary of my accident. I could not move to a beautiful island or spend the summer at a resort, but the serenity garden gave me a place to heal. At peace in this healing place, my reading skills much improved, I could finally read about trauma and grief. This beautiful place I had created gave me a place to dive in to that grief and explore it, to feel it instead of pushing it down with a sense of the need to carry on and be brave. The serenity garden gave me a place I could cry outdoors without the neighbors hearing, the sound (hopefully) overpowered by the sound of the waterfall, the gently moving water that overshadowed the recollection of the cold, bullying whitewater that had threatened to sweep me away, sweep me under. The garden became a manifestation of the serenity I sought to cultivate in my life and the beauty I felt in my heart.

But I didn't stop at the garden. Next I took several sewing classes. It seemed like I may have driven my quilting teacher crazy that my seams weren't perfectly even. I was just so glad I could cut the squares and mostly follow her instructions for putting them together. At home, I drew quilting designs and developed a stash of fabrics whose colors and patterns pleased me. I even made a quilt for a friend's baby. Discerning that I still needed better hand-eye-brain coordination to tackle any more sewing projects, I redecorated several rooms in my home. Pairing drapery fabrics with patterned rugs and wall colors soothed my brain, in addition to creating a space of beauty. Some rooms I re-accessorized or even had my poor husband repaint when my attempts were less successful than I'd hoped. I wanted to try the painting myself, as I'd painted several homes, but although I could roll a wall, I was dangerous with a brush for more than two years as my fine motor skills retuned themselves. I was grateful for the patience my husband practiced even when he didn't feel it. Each project showed me what was healing, what still needed work. There was something about all this left-brain/right-brain coordination that helped me get better.

Rooms in my mind unlocked. I could remember the names and the faces of my high-school classmates. I could remember some of the French I spoke though less of the Spanish and German. I could make a pizza, each week usually more easily than the previous week and eventually as a matter of routine. I designed concrete pathways, a new front porch and retaining walls in the front yard, trimmed with flowerbeds of perennials designed to thrive in the relentless Colorado sun. A neighbor suggested a career as a landscape designer. Friends encouraged a new career as an interior designer. And I considered opening an online décor store with found treasures and handmade objects. I was running out of rooms to redo and the budget to redo them. Money was tight, but the improvements I experienced from these changes were unparalleled by any other aspect of my recovery, by any other set of activities in my life thus far. I needed a way to keep going. While the price of these improvements wasn't inexpensive, it was time to cash in my savings. My rainy day had come and I needed to do whatever I could to get better, lest I be lost to confusion and grief. Bring on the healing. I needed to improve.

Left brain, right brain came together. The front brain, the initiator, planned dozens of smaller projects—a photo calendar, a collage of prints, furniture refinishing. Dozens of projects came into being, some scrapped or thanked for their healing and moved away from. Others now adorn my home's surfaces. The planner, the measurer and the creative genius conspired together. The tactile projects, the ones that put my hands and mind at work together, seemed to yield the most benefits at first and caused the least cognitive fatigue. These were projects I could start and know when they were complete.

Gradually, my recovery time between projects improved. My speech and thinking at the end of a long day were more intact. As my symptoms improved, I focused on the benefits newly attained, never looking back at how I'd been before my accident. The person I'd been before no longer existed.

One day, my therapist suggested I try writing again. I had tried many times, but found it difficult to maintain any one train of thought. I kept a haphazard journal, but only I would see that. My therapist assigned a writing prompt, a way to rewrite the physical pain and awkwardness I felt first thing in the morning, when I "limp-dragged" myself out of bed and down the stairs. My therapist asked me to imagine myself as a goddess waking.

A goddess waking indeed! I wrote a couple of pages that came flowing out of me, coherence, tense and the use of metaphor all present. If I could find those pages now, I suspect I'd find improvements to make and mistakes to correct, but I had written a few pages! That day or that week, I don't remember which, I signed up for a personal narrative workshop. I was never a painter or a dancer. All my life, my medium was writing. I had written short stories and poems, worked as a journalist and editor. Even as a corporate worker, I did all manner of writing, from online learning to video scripts to complex sales proposals. And now I had just written a few pages. I was back! I could write beyond the journal scribblings I'd kept, hoping to piece them into a book to help other people with brain injuries and their loved ones understand what a brain injury can be like by sharing my story with them.

In that first workshop, I sweated in my seat as I tried to make thoughtful comments in class and the life stories just poured out in that wild, uneasy way they can when a writer first turns to personal narrative. I just wanted to think a thought, write it, and then read that same thought on the page. That was my early marker of success.

The tactile projects helped me get sharper. The writing projects helped me sew things together. Personal narrative worked its own healing magic, unburying thoughts, fears and losses stuffed way deep down, buried so deeply they'd become imperceptible in my suited-up corporate adult life. One demon slayed and then another. I was healing more than my brain injury now and letting old defenses crumble. Butterflies of transformation lifted dreams on wings, fluttering, hovering right before me. The gentle whoosh of the butterflies felt medicinal. Their intricately patterned, brightly colored wings swept me into their embrace. I was alive. I was well again. The dark time of healing had been my cocoon.

Eventually, about two years after my accident, my symptoms improved to the point where it was often hard to believe how invasive they had been. Had my accident been that bad? Yes, I had the writing to prove it. A handful of sentences here or there until some other task beckoned or when I backed away emotionally from the topic at hand. As my abilities grew, I wrote pages that took me until the end to identify the subject, but in them I had at least captured the essence—my first time in a boat after my accident, my journals processing the books on trauma and grief I read. Now I was working as a freelance writer and preparing to start the MFA program in creative nonfiction to which I'd recently been accepted. Yes, my husband reminded me, the dark days of my accident had been true, but I was better now.

I'd come a long way from that waking goddess. The creative endeavors I pursued in recovering from my accident empowered me to recognize my own beauty at a time when I was disfigured and felt miserable in my physical body. Those endeavors gave me a sense of purpose. And they served as a skillful guide in navigating the emotional and psychological landscape of my grief and recovery. Being able to pace myself and see where I improved, where I stagnated and where I faltered helped me rediscover confidence in navigating new life choices. Designing a room from start to finish, selling off and donating the items no longer useful and working intimately in the creation of a new space helped me let go of grief and let go of the person I was before my accident. Giving space for the void, knowing that I could replace that void with new life, helped me onward to create the new life of my dreams. Now I flutter my own wings. Now I fly.

"The Goddess Wakes" is a condensed excerpt from my in-progress memoir, *When Someday Came.*

IN RETROSPECT

KAY LEARNED
NORTH TONAWANDA, NY

Recently I found the little journal I kept during my husband's final weeks of life. I had recorded the day-to-day episodes, the ups and downs, the triumphs and defeats, and the ultimate outcome. I was surprised at how many details I'd forgotten. It has been twenty-two years, though, and I think time has a way of making us forget.

When I look back on that time, it's the emotional journey I embarked on afterward that I remember well.

From the start I threw myself into a frantic pace of activity so I didn't have to face the turmoil going on inside me, for Lloyd had been a demanding, controlling, vengeful man during his years of dealing with a brain tumor. As his caregiver, I was his number one enemy, and as a result, I harbored bitterness and self-doubt. It was hard for me to forget the things he'd said to me, or the way he'd acted. Unless I was busy with my hands, I'd replay those things over and over in my brain all day long. Sometimes I'd lose sleep. So frantic activity seemed the only cure. It not only kept my brain busy, I'd be so exhausted I'd sleep well, too. Besides, I felt I couldn't allow myself to get buried emotionally, for I had three children to raise, ages ten, eleven, and fourteen at the time.

The first thing I did was buy a double that needed a lot of TLC. I had this idea that I could renovate the apartments with a little cleaning and a lot of paint. I repeated this project several times over, owning fourteen apartments before I finally got sick of being a landlady and all the problems associated with it. Plus, by the time expenses were paid, I didn't make much money. It just seemed a lot of aggravation for what it was worth. But I believed it served its purpose, for I certainly kept myself at a whirlwind pace.

After a few years I was able to sell off all but one building. It was a mixed-use building, and it had an empty storefront I couldn't get rented. I decided I should start a business and take over the storefront myself. It was something I'd always wanted to do, and the timing seemed right.

I asked a friend if she'd like to come into business with me. We decided we'd sell antiques and gifts out of the empty storefront. I emptied my house of antiques I'd collected over the years, and we purchased our first gift items from Wang's catalogue, COD. We opened our business the first day of February1996.

It was my business partner, Penny, who taught me what it means to set up a display. I was busy arranging things on shelves when she said to me, "I have a better idea. Let me show you."

She walked over to an antique dresser and arranged on top of it an antique lamp, an antique mirror and brush set, a picture frame with a vintage picture, and a Depression glass vase with silk flowers.

When we opened the shop, the first customer not only bought the dresser, she bought everything on it!

Once I saw what happened with that display, I was hooked. It's hard to describe what excitement goes through you when you've just discovered what you want to do for the rest of your life.

When I told Penny how excited I was, she said, "It's the money."

"No, it's a lot more than that," I replied.

From that time on I was able to set up displays and vignettes like I'd been doing it for years, and the thrill of being creative was absolutely exhilarating.

Every summer for Father's Day I took my children to my husband's grave. I felt it was an important part of their staying connected to him.

I'd purchased one of those flat stones that allowed the lawnmower guys to buzz over the top of it with their riding mowers. Because I live in an area with a high water table, the stone sank into the ground after the first year, and grass grew over the top of it. I was disheartened, so every year after that I took a spade with me and cleared away grass and dug a trench around the stone. I filled the trench in with gravel to keep the grass from overtaking it. All my efforts were in vain, though, because each year the stone sank lower and lower, until I thought the earth would swallow it completely.

Five summers ago my son, Luke, now a grown man who lives too far away to join me often, was able to be with me at the grave. We dug around the stone and I pried it up with the spade. He pulled it out of the ground and held it in his arms while I poured a whole bucketful of gravel into the hole. When he replaced the stone, it was way above the ground!

"Terrific," I announced. "If the lawnmower guys drive over it now, they'll be sharpening their blades."

Luke and I got a good laugh out of it.

I still have to dig out grass every year and put gravel around it, but it has never sunk below the ground. I re-outline it, so to speak, so that it shows up in the great manse of flat cemetery stones, many of which have sunk so low they may never be found.

Three summers ago, while standing at Lloyd's grave, I was able, finally, to forgive him and let all my hard feelings go. I knew it was a monumental moment.

Lana, who is the only one of my children who lives close by, comes with me every summer now. She and I talk out loud to my husband while we're there. She tells him things about herself and I tell him things about myself, usually followed by, "If you knew what I did, you'd probably roll over in your grave." We both laugh at the things we say, but since I've made peace with him, I say those things with a certain measure of pride and gratitude.

Back in 2001 Penny and I thought our business would do better if we were in the little downtown section of our city. Even though there were empty storefronts, there seemed to be great potential there. For one thing, the little three-block long, historical strip was surrounded by waterways. And the city had taken the unusual step of spending millions of dollars to put in a new harbor, which was attracting boaters each summer.

We opened a storefront on the street in June of 2001. A few months later 9/11 happened and the bottom fell out of our gift and antique business.

In the meantime, never wanting to give up, I was finally able to sell the multi-use building, and I bought one of the empty storefronts downtown. In June of 2002 we moved into a 3,400 square foot space. Frankly, it was way too big for us and we spent far too much money trying to fill it up.

It took several years of spinning our wheels before we decided we needed to diversify if we were going to survive. So we got a loan and started up a lunch café inside the store. Penny became the manager of the café and I continued managing the retail side of the business. We took on an employee and everything was going well, and then the bottom fell out again in the fall of 2008 with the harsh recession. People stopped buying. Banks stopped lending money. In 2009 our cash flow dwindled to nothing. We fought hard to keep going. It was tough, but in the midst of that financial hardship, I had what I call my epiphany.

When we first moved on the street in 2001, there was an established business that we admired for its success. Joan and Glenna were the owners. They taught art classes, had a frame shop, sold art supplies, and had a gallery. They came to our shop when we first moved in and purchased a few items. Penny asked them what they were going to do with what they purchased and Glenna said, "We're going to put these items in a set-up and paint them. You need to come see us. I bet you two would be good artists. I can tell by the way you display things."

The following week we took Joan and Glenna up on their invitation and toured their facility. They showed us the gallery first, where local artists had displayed their works. Next they showed us the studio. We watched people seated at easels, with a "set-up" in front of them, painting in oils. The smell of the paint and turpentine had a pull on me that was electrifying. I couldn't wait to begin. Penny and I signed up for art classes right away.

I thought I was going to show up at class and immediately get to paint. But that was not the case. Joan had her own system of teaching and I was her student.

"You have to learn to draw before you can paint," she said. "And your drawings have to meet my standards of excellence before you graduate to the next level."

"Okay," I said. She could have told me to stand on my head and I would have done it.

I was given a beginner kit with different sizes of graphite, a small ruler, and a kneadable erasure. I was put in front of a set-up and told to start.

"Draw what you see," she said.

After three hours of working my butt off, she stood behind me again.

"Is that what you see?" she asked.

Obviously my first attempt at drawing had failed.

After months of hard work, she finally told me I could graduate to the next level.

"Can I paint now?" I asked excitedly.

"Nope, now you have to learn to use pastels."

Many months later I was finally allowed to graduate to painting. Once I started, I knew I was in love. The three-hour long class each week became my escape. During those three hours I felt like a canopy of peace surrounded me. I was in a zone where nothing bothered me and nothing could touch me. There were no thoughts of Lloyd, no stresses about kids, no worries about finances. In that zone the sun shone brightly all around me.

Now many years later, Penny and I still take art lessons. Our paintings hang all around our shop. In fact, the café walls are lined with our works. We've both sold paintings right off the wall. Nowadays I paint mostly local scenes. I put my own spin on the scene by way of lighting and coloring. Most importantly, people respond favorably to my work. I've had prints made from the originals and I sell them as cards and plaques, and they sell very well.

Another thing I've done is make replicas of historical buildings in our area. I form the building out of cardboard first, then coat it with paper Mache and paint it. These buildings sit on top of display units all over the retail side. At Christmas I put them in the window and create a Christmas village. It's fun to watch people stop in front of the window and smile with recognition of what they're seeing.

One day when Penny and I were in the midst of our 2009 financial woes, I said to her, "We'll probably be poor the rest of our lives because of this business, but we're creating art. Don't you see? That's what it's all about. I think I'm happier than I've ever been. It must be because I'm being what God created me to be."

Then I said, "I think that was my epiphany!"

It took awhile for me to put two and two together, but I'm sure it's why I was able to forgive Lloyd. Understanding that I could be happy just being what God created me to be freed me from my bitterness. I no longer needed to store my grievances in the file cabinets of my brain. I could let it all go. I had found myself.

Now, after re-reading my journal entries from twenty-two years ago, I'm able to see things differently. My feelings no longer get in the way. I'm able to see what awful things Lloyd went through, how awful it must have been for him to know he was dying at age forty-two, and with three young children.

I still can't imagine it, really. I can't imagine what it would be like to know I was dying now, at age sixty-five, having had time to live my life and fulfill my dreams. I've seen my kids grow up and become independent and marry and have kids of their own. I've seen five sweet and beautiful grandchildren come into the world. I'm enjoying all my creative projects, and I've seen our business grow on a street that has finally become a destination. (In just the last couple years investors have poured millions into transforming empty buildings. Now there are upscale apartments, a yoga studio, a juice bar, new restaurants and boutiques. Empty storefronts are a thing of the past.)

My husband never got to see his dreams fulfilled, not any of them. He never got to see his kids graduate from high school and go to college. He never got to watch a daughter walk across the stage and be given the title of doctor. He never got to walk a daughter down the aisle at her wedding. He never got to be in the delivery room when a grandchild was born and hold that child minutes after its birth.

I don't know what it would have been like to grow old with him. The last years of our marriage were consumed with surgeries and doctors and grand mal seizures and Dilantin and radiation and chemotherapy. Unfortunately, those things crowded out the good memories.

So I ask myself now; would we have enjoyed being sixty-something together? I'd like to think so. But would he have allowed me to do the things I've done—own my own business, manage my own finances, and spend long hours painting? I'd like to think so, and I'd like to think he would've enjoyed my art.

Maybe along the way we would've traveled together, and played more tennis. Maybe we would've competed in more mixed-doubles tournaments.

At any rate, I'm terribly sorry that he missed so much of life. He desperately wanted to live, that much I know. He pushed the envelope, trying to have another surgery just months after his last one. He hung onto the hope that another surgery would prolong his life, even for just a few more months. It didn't, of course. That surgery left him unable to speak or swallow.

Shortly after the surgery a blood clot formed in his leg. The doctors were unable to give him blood thinner because it would've caused his brain to bleed. The blood clot moved to his lungs and he fought to breathe. In the middle of the night, it moved to his heart.

He died a mere four days after the surgery. Had he lived his few months more, I don't think he would've been happy. The doctors had already warned me he was going to need a feeding tube and around-the-clock nursing care.

At first people asked me if I was going to marry again. A friend even called to insist I should remarry. I think people should not ask questions like that and force their opinions on a widow or widower. I told people the answer was no. My children didn't want me to bring a stepfather into the equation, and my initial hurt and bitterness made it impossible to consider. Besides, once I tasted independence, I knew there was no turning back.

Some women need a man to make their lives complete. I found I didn't. I've enjoyed having my own ideas about God and about politics, and those ideas are very different from what Lloyd's were. (See, he really would roll over in his grave!)

When I re-read that little journal I kept, I felt deep regret that I'd been so consumed with myself that I'd been unable to see the whole picture. I regret never having told Lloyd that he was a very brave man, that he fought an unbelievable battle against an awful disease and never gave up hope, never gave up wanting to live. Most of all I regret not having more empathy and understanding for him when he needed it the most.